Christmas 2003.

Hope you enjoy reading
this book Sue

Love Viv and John

Good Housekeeping

herb book

Good Housekeeping

how to grow
and cook with
herbs successfully

herb book

Jane Eastoe

Special Photography
Carol Sharp

HarperCollins*Publishers*

First published in 2002 by
HarperCollinsPublishers
77–85 Fulham Palace Road
London W6 8JB

The HarperCollins website address is:
www.**fire**and**water**.com

05 04 03 02 01 00
9 8 7 6 5 4 3 2 1

Published in association with The National Magazine Company Limited
Good Housekeeping is a registered trade mark of
The National Magazine Company Limited

The Good Housekeeping website address is:
www.goodhousekeeping.co.uk

The expression Good Housekeeping as used in the title of the book is
the mark of the National Magazine Company Limited and the Hearst
Corporation, registered in the United Kingdom and the USA, and other
principal countries in the world, and is the absolute property of the National
Magazine Company and the Hearst Corporation. The use of this trade mark
other than with the express permission of the National Magazine Company
Limited or the Hearst Corporation is strictly prohibited.

A CIP catalogue record for this book is available from the British Library

ISBN: 0 00 713946 2

Colour reproduction by Dot Gradations
Printed and bound in the UK by Bath Press

This book is typeset in Helvetica, HelveticaNeue and Eurostile

Contents

Foreword

There are so many wonderful herbs now available in the supermarkets, food markets and fruit and vegetable shops that you may be wondering why go to the trouble of growing your own. Firstly, it's so easy and convenient to go into the garden or to your kitchen windowsill and pick your own; secondly, of course, it's cheaper than buying them. Nor do you need a huge garden to start growing herbs. Basil, for instance, grows brilliantly in pots and will flourish in a sunny spot. But if you do have more space, this book shows you how to cultivate a variety of herbs.

The first section of the book deals with the practicalities. Find out what type of soil is in your garden to discover the best herbs to grow there. There are hints and tips as to how to deal with pests and diseases and how to turn waste into useful matter by making a compost heap. Plus there's information on the best time to harvest your herbs.

The rest of the book deals with the amazing array of herbs that you can grow – from the ubiquitous parsley, garlic, rocket and basil to the more unusual types like borage, myrtle, sweet woodruff and liquorice – their medicinal uses and how to cook with them. Consider using crab apples to make wonderful jelly; hops, favoured by the Italians, taste great in a simple omelette while scented geraniums make a pretty statement in a salad. So with that taster – what are you waiting for? Enjoy!

Emma Marsden

Emma Marsden
Deputy Cookery Editor
Good Housekeeping

Introduction

Herbs have been used in daily life for centuries and for good reason: they transform the flavour of food, are packed with nutrients, are beneficial to our health, are useful around the home and can even help improve our appearance. It is one of the tragedies of modern life, therefore, that as we wholeheartedly embrace consumerism we have lost many of the skills and much of the knowledge about herbs that were taken for granted by our forebears for centuries.

We also seem to be failing to establish the essential connection between our current twin passions of cooking and gardening. A gardener may grow herbs because they are pretty, but rarely use them in the home. On the other hand an enthusiastic gourmet who laments the limited selection of fresh herbs on offer in the supermarket may never think of cultivating them. Nor may it occur to the tea drinker who consumes quantities of dried herb to try the fresh leaves and flowers growing on the doorstep. And for those of us who despair at our inability to treat even minor ailments ourselves, safe home-made herbal remedies could so easily bring relief. The solution open to everyone is to cultivate and use herbs according to their requirement. It is so staggeringly easy that once embarked upon it rapidly becomes a way of life.

What is a herb?

A herb can be loosely defined as any plant whose leaves are used for food, scent or medicine. Many thousands of plants fit into this classification, ranging from popular culinary herbs like the parsley, sage, rosemary and thyme of ballad fame to highly toxic plants like foxglove, poppy and yew – respectively sources of the heart drug digitalis, the painkiller morphine and the cancer treatment taxol.

The way to good health

Herbs are powerhouses of vitamins, nutrients and minerals. Not only do they flavour food, transforming the simplest of meals into a culinary delight, they also bring enormous health benefits. Many herbs are excellent digestive aids, assisting our body in dealing with overly rich food;

others are cleansing and help the liver and kidneys function efficiently. Increasing daily consumption of culinary herbs will boost health and vitality, greatly enhancing the body's ability to combat stress, viruses and infections.

Treating ailments

Alternative therapies, such as homeopathy and herbalism, have long recognised the power of plants, but it is only now that science is undertaking serious research into the healing properties of herbs and looking at the scientific basis of traditional remedies. Even sceptical doctors now acknowledge that herbs have great medicinal potential. In the home, herbs can be used to alleviate or treat the symptoms of many common complaints – from colds, cystitis, sore throats and indigestion to chilblains.

A nice cup of tea

Fresh herb teas can be drunk for pleasure, to soothe and relax as well as to treat specific ailments. They bear no resemblance to commercial herb teas, so if those are not to your taste do not be put off.

Growing your own

The flavour of home-grown, freshly picked herbs is infinitely superior to what is on offer elsewhere – many supermarket plants are grown hydroponically, which results in less flavour. Also, as the retail choice is limited, if you want a fresh supply of more interesting herbs, the only option is to grow your own.

Ethereal pleasure

Herbs are satisfyingly easy to cultivate, and intrinsically therapeutic. They are

subtle, pretty and soothing, and a designated herb bed is often the most tranquil
area of any garden. Their delightful fragrances can also be introduced into the
home in many ways.

About this book

This book will show you how to grow and
use your own supply of fresh herbs, no
matter how limited your space may be.
The directory provides detailed information
on 65 herbs, including historical back-
ground, cultivation advice and suggestions
for medicinal, culinary, household and
cosmetic use. There are recipes for the
kitchen, the sick room and the bathroom.
The herbs are listed alphabetically by their
botanical Latin names, but if you know
only the common name, look for it in the
index at the back of the book.

Advice

Herbs are powerful plants. Many are toxic
or can be safely used for only short periods of time. However, they are no different
from many other commonly used substances such as alcohol or chocolate,
which can also be damaging if taken to
excess. We all know that one aspirin a
day will thin the blood, two can ease a
headache, but exceeding the recommended dose can be life threatening.
Similarly, herbs must treated with respect
and used sensibly; it would certainly be
foolish to attempt to treat anything other
than minor complaints. If in doubt about
any health matter always consult your
general practitioner and seek guidance
from a qualified herbalist. If you are pregnant or using any form of medication seek
advice before taking a herbal preparation.

Herbs through History

There is plenty of evidence that man has recognised and utilised the powerful properties of herbs for thousands of years. Of the eight species of plants found in the grave of a Neanderthal man in Shanidar Cave in Iraq, six – yarrow, horsetail, hollyhock, St. Barnaby's thistle, cornflower and grape hyacinth – are still used medicinally today. The earliest dated written material includes Assyrian clay tablets from c. 2500BC and The Ebers papyrus, c. 2000BC, on which ancient Egyptians recorded over 800 remedies, many utilising herbs. Herbs are also frequently mentioned in the Bible, the Torah and the Koran and have featured in folklore and legend across the world and throughout history.

Early use

Man's use of herbs for food, medicine and cosmetics stretches back long before written records began. As a hunter-gatherer, man would have been using herbs since his earliest days. Finding out what was safe to eat must have been a matter of trial and error, doubtless with fatalities along the way, but over time a body of knowledge was built up and passed down through the generations by word of mouth.

The powerful properties possessed by many herbs were clearly recognised, but not understood and certain plants became the subject of much superstition and mysticism – how else could the hallucinogenic visions produced by eating a certain berry or bark be explained?

Recording for posterity

Over the centuries herbs became a part of everyday life, used for food, medicines, dyes, disinfectants, cosmetics and perfumes. Indeed they were so important that they were the subject of many early writings. These works were of significance, for instead of relying on word of mouth the characteristics of plants were being carefully recorded for future reference. The *Canon of Herbs*, one of the earliest Chinese herbals, details 252 plant medications. It is attributed to the Chinese emperor Shen Nong, who lived around 3000BC. He noted the effect of various herbs after acting as a human guinea pig.

At the same time writers were noting information about herb perfumes, cosmetics and flower essences. Cosmetics and fragrances played an important role in many ancient religious ceremonies and were significant in the embalming process; chamomile oil was used to embalm the mummy of Rameses II, who died in 1224BC. The Egyptians, in particular, developed many toiletries from plants, including creams and depilatory waxes.

The ancient Greeks were the first to expound modern concepts of health and beauty. In 400BC, the physician and teacher, Hippocrates, wrote about the value and use of herbs as pain relief and treatment. The historian, Herodotus, writing in 500BC, named over 700 plants in common use.

Scattering seed

The Roman Empire was responsible for introducing many Mediterranean plants to its conquered territories. The Romans imported some 200 species of herb to Britain, amongst them borage, fennel, parsley, sage, rosemary and thyme. The spread of the papacy into the former Roman territories, from AD600 onwards, was significant in the development of herb gardens and the practice of medicine. The monastic movement originated in Egypt, where some Christian converts felt that a full Christian lifestyle was incompatible with earthly pleasures. They withdrew from the world, building walls around their communities and gardens within – self-sufficiency was essential to their way of life. Thus the pattern for the cloistered lifestyle and its horticultural emphasis was established.

The source of much of the herbal medicine practised by the Christian religious orders in medieval Europe is believed to have been *Materia Medica*, produced in the first century AD by the Greek physician Dioscorides. One of the earliest herbals, it details the medical

properties of over 500 herbs Dioscorides deemed useful to the human species and effectively became a standard textbook, as well as a prototype for all future work. By AD1000 monks like William of Dijon had established reputations as skilled physicians. At the same time infirmaries began to appear in monasteries with herb, or physic (medicinal), gardens sited alongside. Monks continued to practise medicine throughout most of the Middle Ages.

Day-to-day essentials

Herbs at this time were used principally to flavour food, to act as a preservative and to ease flatulence. Many herbs are cited as bringing digestive relief, but when you think about the quality of the food being consumed in those pre-refrigerator, grow-your-own, slaughter-your-own days you understand better the need for soothing remedies. Many were taken in the form of infusions and cordials, and herbs were commonly added to beer and wines, which were developed by the monks as a digestive aid for consumption during and after meals. Aniseed, hyssop and liquorice were significant ingredients in many early beers, liqueurs and spirits and were utilised as much for their digestive properties as for their distinctive flavouring.

Decorative posturing

The influence from Europe in medieval Britain was significant. Of 22 Queens of England between 1066 and 1485 only five were born in the country. Many brought gardeners with them, although in times of war gardens came second to defence and many were destroyed. The real development of herb gardens came in the fifteenth and sixteenth centuries. It was a time of relative peace and security, when peasants were free to work the land and noblemen signalled their wealth and power by building grand homes and gardens instead of fighting their neighbours. There was a new interest in gardens and cooking amongst the landed gentry, who sought to copy the formal designs found in monasteries. This influence is believed to have developed from the original Egyptian monastery gardens, which were inspired in turn by the classic Persian foursquare garden.

Knot gardens were the fashion and ever more intricate designs were created, with the herbs contained therein often for ornament rather than use. It was in the kitchen gardens of both peasants and the nobility that herbs were grown for culinary and physic (medicinal) use.

Exploring use

In AD77 the Roman writer Pliny produced the first herbal. Known as *Natural History*, it was a dictionary of simple drugs. This encyclopaedic work expounded the original concept of the Doctrine of Signatures, suggesting that the characteristics and appearance of a plant gave clues to its possible use. The German physician Paracelus explored this idea further in his influential herbal published in 1570. The approach may seem fanciful and certainly unscientific by modern standards, but, curiously, many of the plants listed do

indeed function medicinally as he suggested. For example, the use of willow, which grows in damp and cold conditions, was proposed as treatment for rheumatic complaints caused by cold damp conditions. Willow is a rich source of salicylic acid and from it, in 1899, a German chemist developed acetyl-salicylic acid, which is the basis of aspirin.

Herbals

During the sixteenth and seventeenth centuries, many new works were published. William Turner (1510–68) was the first person to attempt to name and classify native British plants, which suggested a new source of herbal material. John Gerard (1545–1612), an apothecary to James I, produced his *Herball* in 1597 and personally grew over 1000 species in his garden. John Parkinson detailed some 3000 species in his *Theatrum Botanicum* in 1629. Nicholas Culpeper (1616–54) followed on with *The English Physician* in 1652. It was much ridiculed at the time as it made much of the astrological aspects of plants as well as their medicinal properties, diminishing his credibility. However, he effected so many cures that doctors claimed he must have used witchcraft.

In 1569 Nicholas Monardes, a Spanish doctor, published the earliest known American herbal. He listed many of the plants taken out by the settlers, who relied on fast-growing herbs, such as sorrel and Good King Henry (*Chenopodium bonus-henricus*), or those packed with nutrients, such as parsley, to restore good health

quickly. Monardes also noted the native plants, such as bergamot, which the native Americans used to make a form of tea. Red bergamot (*Monarda didyama*) is named after him.

Personal records

In the seventeenth century stillroom books joined herbals in recording the day-to-day use of herbs: recipes, remedies and advice were noted down to be passed from one generation to the next. The family matriarch, who had a lifetime of experience in dealing with all matters relating to the family's health and welfare, maintained these documents. The name originates from the presence of the still – an essential piece of household equipment, where spirits and floral waters could be distilled.

Studying medicine

At the same time, advances in scientific understanding ensured that plants were being properly classified and dissected. Every university of note had its own physic garden, where botany and medicine were taught side by side. Herbs were grown in alphabetical sequence for ease of reference. Little by little, scientists were able to extract plant components to produce formulaic extracts, and by the eighteenth century the study of botany and medicine was separating into two distinct sciences.

Growth curtailed

As the Industrial Revolution got under way, the pattern of life began to change – people moved from the country and sought work in the cities. Housing sprang up where there was little or no room to grow any plants. Old-fashioned remedies were abandoned in favour of proprietary treatments and gradually centuries-old skills were forgotten or recalled only as fantastical old wives' tales.

In fact, it was in Britain alone that the use of herbs so dramatically declined. In all other European countries the domestic kitchen-garden cultivation of herbs continued unabated. Herbs grew vigorously in the wild, and commercial cultivation of them was widespread. Dried herbs were then imported to Britain for both culinary and medicinal use but the quality was poor and the use of all herbs, bar the parsley, sage, rosemary and thyme of folksong fame, declined.

Old wives' tales

In the twentieth century, advances in scientific knowledge enabled scientists to isolate the chemical properties of a plant and synthesise it. It became possible to produce accurate doses of drugs that were readily available from the chemist. It was not until the First World War that people began to use the old remedies again and only then because they were driven to it by acute shortages of both food and medicine. Women began to cultivate herbs for their nutritional content, while soldiers in the trenches began using garlic, thyme and moss to help save lives when they ran out of conventional treatments. Lavender was gathered and its oil used as a surgical antiseptic in field hospitals.

Nettle, which is rich in vitamins, nutrients and notably iron, was given to wounded soldiers as a tonic. In 1931 Mrs M. Grieve produced *A Modern Herbal*, which detailed over 1000 plants. It proved almost as popular as Culpeper's writings and generated new interest in the subject.

Culinary use

In writing about the history of herbs it is easy to sound as though their only significance was in the area of medicine. However, even in culinary terms herbs are naturally beneficial – they are packed with nutrients, vitamins and minerals. Their qualities as flavourings have been an integral part of good cooking since ancient times. An early cookery book, written by the Roman gourmet Apicus in AD27–37, details many unusual herb combinations. In the sixteenth century Thomas Tusser, a steward who produced the exhaustive reference book *Five Hundred Pointes of Good Husbandry*, recommended planting some 70 salad and potherbs in his kitchen-garden plan for farmers' wives. Herbs were used daily in salads, indeed there were potherbs for use in the cooking pot and salad herbs for use as fresh leaf – the term 'vegetable' did not come into general use until the nineteenth century.

The characteristic basis of the much-admired French cuisine was established in the eighteenth and nineteenth centuries after the French revolution. The ostentatious gastronomic excesses of the royal court were abandoned in favour of simple, well-cooked, seasonal food. Wherever possible fruit, vegetables and salad ingredients were picked fresh. It is with just this school of cookery that the addition of a few well-chosen culinary herbs makes the world of difference to flavour – using plants in just the right quantities to complement the taste of the food. And it is with the ingenious use of herbs that many modern chefs are establishing their reputations – for nothing excites the jaded modern palette more than a whole new taste experience.

The way forward

There has been a dramatic revival in the interest in herbs over the last 40 years. In the 1960s cooks began to rediscover long-forgotten herbs. Since then consumers have turned to supposedly natural products. There has been a kickback against the vast profits made by cosmetic companies and the consumer is looking for more environmentally friendly products. Scientists have now begun to undertake serious research into the properties offered by many different plants. Pharmaceutical companies are also investing vast sums of money in research projects in the hope of producing a new and profitable wonder drug.

This research is in its infancy when you consider that of some 25,000 listed plant species around 2500 have traditionally been used for medicinal purposes. To date, only around 250 of these have been subject to serious investigation to find a scientific explanation for their reputed effects. Herbs have a long way to go yet!

growing herbs

Propagating Herbs

sowing seed outdoors

1 Mark out the seed drill (the narrow furrow in the soil where seeds are sown) with pegs and string. Using this line, create a shallow drill with the corner of a hoe or rake.

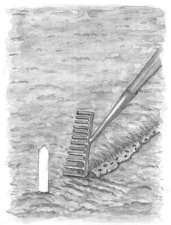

2 Scatter the seeds in the drill and cover them with soil using the back of the hoe or rake. Gently firm the soil with the back of the rake.

Anyone can go out and buy a new plant for the garden, but purchasing herbs can be expensive if you want several plants. Also, if you are looking for something rather unusual you may find it is not locally available and you might be disappointed. The solution is to propagate the plants yourself.

Fortunately, many herbs are easy and satisfying to propagate – by seed, cuttings, division or layering – so do not be daunted by what might at first appear to be complicated intricacies. Sowing seeds, pricking out and transplanting or nurturing delicate cuttings may seem complicated as well as time-consuming in our busy modern lives, but they do not have to be. Once you understand how the different methods of propagation work you can make decisions as to which are best suited to the plants you want to grow or reproduce. Success will depend on giving new plants a good start, as well as being realistic about the amount of time you are able to devote to propagation.

Seed

Growing plants from seed is a pleasing activity. It is nature at its most basic. Seeds are programmed to remain dormant until a specific set of conditions stimulates germination; all that most need are water, air and warmth, and occasionally light. Before you plan extravagant planting schemes and buy masses of seed, however, think carefully about how much time and space you can realistically devote to this method of propagation, especially if you wish to sow indoors.

As a matter of principle, I never sow indoors if the herb can withstand being sown directly into the ground. There is no choice with those herbs that resent their roots being disturbed and so react badly to being transplanted; these should always be sown directly into the garden, even if you have to wait until later in the season when the soil is warmer. The advantage of

sowing indoors, where you can provide extra warmth if necessary and protection from wind and damp, is that this allows crops to develop earlier; the disadvantage is that plants grown this way require more time and effort. Some half-hardy or tender plants can only be sown indoors: for instance, basil seedlings tend to rot in a damp northern climate and sweet marjoram seeds are so small they are better started off in a pot.

Seed packets contain much useful information, so always check the back for specific instructions on how to sow the herb they contain.

Stratification

Some seeds have evolved to survive the periods of warmth and/or cold that may occur in their indigenous environment prior to the time when conditions for their germination are suitable. To overcome this

it will be necessary to mimic the natural climatic events in an accelerated fashion. This can be done by first placing the seeds in a bag of sand and leaf-mould and storing them at temperatures of 20–25ºC (68–77ºF) for four to 12 weeks. The bag must then be transferred to a refrigerator for a further four to 12 weeks, after which the seeds can be sown in a seed tray. Some seeds may need to be soaked overnight to soften the surface before this treatment. Primroses, violets, sweet woodruff and sweet cicely all benefit from a period of stratification.

Outdoor sowing

Most herbs can be safely sown directly into the garden from mid- to late spring. Prepare your seed bed in autumn by either digging in organic matter or applying it as mulch. The cold weather allows the soil to break down the nutrients in the organic

sowing seed indoors

1 Scatter the seeds on top of a pot. If the seeds are very small use a thin piece of folded cardboard to control distribution. Place some seeds inside the fold and tap gently to release them over the compost.

2 Cover the seeds with sieved compost or perlite, according to the instructions on the seed packet.

3 Stand the pot in a bowl of water until the surface of the compost is damp; this is better for the seeds than watering from above.

matter into a form that is accessible to plants. Finish by raking the soil well in spring. Mark a line with string and make a seed drill 5–10mm (¼–½in) deep. Sow the seeds at a rate of two or three per 2.5cm (1in). Thin out seedlings when they reach 5–10cm (2–4in); if you allow the plants to grow overcrowded they will become leggy and prone to disease.

Indoor sowing

Seed can be started off in a greenhouse if you want the plants to get under way early, or if you want to grow unusual or tender specimens. Do not be tempted to sow seed too early in the season or the seedlings will get leggy while you wait for weather that is sufficiently warm for them to be hardened off and planted outside. Most seeds germinate best at around 18–21°C (65–70°F) but if you do not own a greenhouse, a thermostatically con-

trolled windowsill propagator is very efficient. Even a piece of Perspex or glass laid over the top of a seed tray kept on a windowsill will prove very effective.

All seed trays and pots should be thoroughly cleaned before use to help minimise the spread of pests and diseases. Select a suitable growing medium; sterile seed compost is always best, as garden compost generally contains weed seeds. If necessary sieve the compost until it has a fine texture with no lumps; this allows water to be drawn up through the soil by capillary action to give the seeds the moisture they require. Do not allow seed trays to dry out, or to become waterlogged. The latter can cause damping off disease – a fungal infection that will kill off the seedlings.

Some seeds, like foxglove and chamomile, must have light to germinate – indeed very few seeds can germinate in

complete darkness only. They should be sown directly on to the surface of the seed tray. Others can be scattered on the surface of the tray and covered with a fine layer of compost or other growing medium such as vermiculite or perlite. Vermiculite and perlite (granules of volcanic material) are often recommended for sowing herb seeds as these materials allow the free passage of air, water and some light through the surface of the soil, as well as offering a sterile surface growing medium, which is less prone to harbouring disease. Larger seeds such as sunflowers, may be pressed into the compost. Very small seeds can be very difficult to sow and tend to stick to hands and fingers. To avoid this, fold a piece of cardboard or stiff paper in half, place the seeds in the fold and gently tap to distribute the seed. If the seed is mixed with a little silver sand it makes them even easier to handle.

softwood, greenwood and semi-ripe cuttings

1 Prepare all pots and compost in advance as the sooner the cutting is planted the more likely it is to succeed. Using secateurs, take a cutting a little below a leaf joint.

2 Using a sharp knife, make a cleaner cut immediately below the leaf joint, then remove the lower leaves.

3 Push the cutting into prepared compost then water. Semi-ripe cuttings benefit from having a thin layer of sharp sand at the top of the pot so that when the cutting is placed into the pot only the base sits in the growing medium.

pricking out

1 Gently lever the seedlings out of the growing medium, using a pencil or a spoon. Hold the seedling by a leaf and not its stem.

2 Transfer the seedling to a larger pot to grow on.

Pricking out seedlings

Prick out the seedlings when they are large enough to handle and transfer them to a larger container. Keep them in the warm environment until they start to grow on. The plants should then be gradually hardened off – that is placed outside in the daytime for increasing amounts of time and graduating to nights in a cold frame – so that they become acclimatised. After a couple of weeks they can be planted out in the garden.

Cuttings

Taking cuttings is an effective way to multiply existing plants and can be far less time-consuming than growing from seed. There are basically four different types of cuttings, depending on where you cut and at what time of the year: softwood, greenwood or semi-ripe, hardwood and root. Always use a knife to take cuttings as scissors will seal the end of the cut stem and so discourage root growth. Adhering to this rule will make a big difference to the number of cuttings that root successfully. Many gardeners use a hormone-rooting powder when taking cuttings; this encourages root development but can be dispensed with, especially if you want to garden organically. The cuttings will take root without any such assistance.

Softwood cuttings

These cuttings are taken from the tips of new shoots in spring. The young material takes root readily, but as the cuttings are susceptible to moisture loss they tend to be most successful in the controlled conditions of a greenhouse or cool house. Spray leaves frequently in hot, dry weather.

Greenwood and semi-ripe cuttings

Greenwood cuttings are taken in early to mid-summer from, as the name suggests, young green wood. These cuttings take longer to root than softwood cuttings, but are more resilient. Similarly, semi-ripe cuttings, taken in late summer, are less prone to wilt. As with softwood cuttings, both forms do best under controlled conditions.

hardwood cuttings

Put grit or sharp sand in the bottom of a narrow V-shaped trench. Take cuttings with at least three buds, making the top cut level and the bottom one angled. Place the cuttings in the trench with one bud above the surface then fill with soil.

root cuttings

1 Choose small lateral roots (a side growth from a root) for cuttings. Trim each section so that you have a straight cut across the top and an angled or slanting cut at the bottom; this helps you plant the cutting the right way up.

2 Place the cuttings in compost so that the top of each root is level with the surface of the compost, then cover with a thin layer of fine gravel or perlite.

division

1 Lift the plant that is to be divided out of the soil, then split into two using one or two forks to gently separate the root system. Alternatively, cut the root ball in two using a sharp knife. Replant each section.

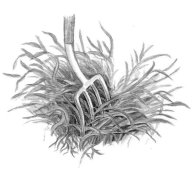

Hardwood cuttings

Cuttings from mature hardwood are taken at the end of the growing season, any time between autumn and spring. These are the easiest cuttings to maintain but are very slow to root.

Root cuttings

Root cuttings are taken from young vigorous roots when the plant is dormant, usually between autumn and spring. Dig up the plant and cut off 5–10cm (2–4in) sections of root, ensuring that each piece contains a growing bud. Place the root sections in a pot of compost and cover with a further 2.5cm (1in) of compost. This very easy method of propagation is particularly suited to plants with spreading roots, such as mint, bergamot, violet and sweet woodruff.

Division

Many perennial plants benefit from being lifted and divided every few years and herbs are no exception. As well as providing new plants, this checks spread and encourages fresh growth. Division is best undertaken when the plant is dormant, usually in autumn or early spring. Simply dig up the plant and carefully separate it into several flowering portions. Replant each section and water. The new plants should soon start to grow. Chives, lemon balm, violet, thyme, lovage and marjoram are good candidates for division.

Layering

Another method of propagating herbs is by layering. This method encourages root development by covering a portion of stem with soil while it is still attached to the parent plant. Suitable candidates for layering are rosemary, sage and bay. If you want to propagate using this method, prune back a few low branches during the winter months to encourage strong spring growth. Trim leaves and side shoots from a healthy branch between 10 and 50cm (4–20in) from the growing tip. Bring the stem down to the soil and peg in place so that the growing tip is vertical. If the soil is in poor condition you could add some compost and grit. Keep the growing tip well watered. The following autumn liberate the plant from its parent, but let it remain where it has taken root for a full year before transplanting.

layering

Trim the leaves and side shoots from a low-growing healthy branch and anchor it in the soil with a peg, ensuring that the growing tip is upright. Leave in place for at least one year.

Taking cuttings

Type of cutting	Time of year	Method	Growing medium	Care	Time to root	Suitable plants
Softwood	Spring	Cut fresh, young growth from the plant and trim cleanly just below a node (leaf joint). Remove leaves from the bottom third of the cutting	50% bark, 50% potting compost	Put the cuttings in a propagator, heated or unheated; you can use a plastic bag if you turn it inside out regularly to prevent moisture build-up, and keep the plastic away from the leaves. Spray the plants daily	2–4 weeks	Lavender, marjoram, mint, rosemary, rue, sage, tarragon, thyme
Greenwood or semi-ripe	Mid-summer to mid-autumn	Cut fresh, young growth from the plant and trim cleanly just below a node (leaf joint). Remove leaves from the bottom third of the cutting	Mix of grit or perlite, potting compost and bark in equal parts	Place in a cold greenhouse or cold frame until spring and take care not to over water. Harden off young plants in spring	4–6 weeks	Shrubby herbs: elder, juniper, lavender, myrtle, rosemary and thyme
Hardwood	Mid- to late autumn	Cut fresh, young growth from the plant and trim cleanly just below a node (leaf joint). Remove leaves from the bottom third of the cutting	Mix of grit or perlite, potting compost and bark in equal parts	Place in a cold frame, greenhouse or conservatory until rooted	Up to 1 year	Box, honeysuckle, rose and rue
Root	Spring or autumn	Cut a 5–8cm (2–3in) piece of root, with a growing bud where visible, and plant vertically	Mix of bark and potting compost in equal parts	Place in a cold frame, greenhouse or conservatory until rooted. Do not water until top growth appears. Harden off when rooted and plant out in spring	2–3 weeks	Plants with creeping root systems: chamomile, comfrey, horseradish, lemon balm and mint

Cultivating Herbs

Herbs are obligingly easy plants to cultivate. They are sturdy and disease resistant, and many will self-seed freely given the right growing conditions. Although the plants are largely undemanding, if you take a little time to cultivate a suitable environment for them to grow in, they will respond and you will be rewarded with abundant crops that will provide for all your requirements.

First you need to establish precisely what type of soil you have in the garden then work accordingly. For example, incorporating a little sand and grit to improve drainage, feeding a sandy soil with some organic matter or raising or lowering the pH balance (the level of acidity) of the soil could make the world of difference to productivity. Thorough weed eradication prior to planting and laying mulch to deter further weed spread will prove a labour-saving device and promote vigorous plant growth. Making your own compost recycles garden waste and provides a steady supply of nutritious and soil-enhancing organic matter.

Herbs that are used as part of a garden's design, such as clipped hedges, topiary and even areas of lawn, will need care and attention to keep them looking their best at all times.

Soil

Good soil is the starting point in all areas of gardening, so if you want to get the best from your herbs you should assess the condition of the soil before you tackle the planting. Soil is graded according to its clay, silt and sand content. The size and ratio of these mineral particles affect the behaviour of the soil. Loam soils have the perfect combination of mineral particle sizes with around 10–25 per cent clay – a mix that offers high fertility with good drainage and water retention. All soils can be improved with soil additives such as garden compost, manure and lime. You can determine the kind of soil you are working by simply rubbing it in your hands.

Clay

Soil that is sticky and greasy and will roll into a ball in the hand is clay. It is heavy, slow draining and slow to warm up in spring, but usually has a high nutrient content. The fine particles are easily compacted and damaged, however, so it should not be worked when wet. Herbs will grow readily in clay, but if you incorporate sand or coarse grit and organic matter on an annual basis this will gradually improve the condition of the soil. When planting Mediterranean herbs throw a few handfuls of coarse grit or gravel into the planting hole to improve drainage.

Chalk

A chalky soil feels crumbly and powdery to the touch. It is shallow and stony but is moderately fertile and free draining and has the advantage of warming up quickly in the spring. However, it is by nature alkaline and as most herbs prefer neutral soil it may be necessary to try to raise the pH balance (*see page 22*) in order to grow a wider range of useful plants.

Sand

A soil that feels gritty is sandy. Its large particles give a light, dry free-draining soil that is easy to work but not very fertile. Many herbs, notably those indigenous to the Mediterranean region, enjoy this type of soil because it is never too wet and warms up very quickly in spring. You can improve sandy soil by incorporating organic matter to help it retain moisture and nutrients. You may need to irrigate frequently during dry weather.

Silt

A silt soil feels soapy or silky to the touch. It is more fertile and moisture retentive than sandy soil, but is also more easily damaged by compaction. As it retains more nutrients than sandy soil and warms up quickly in spring, many herbs will thrive in it.

PH balance

The pH balance of a soil is a measure of its acidity or alkalinity, on a scale of 1–14. A pH reading below 7 indicates an acid soil, while a pH reading over 7 indicates an alkaline soil. Herbs do best in a fairly neutral soil with a pH balance of between 6.5 and 7.5. If your soil is very acid you will need to raise the pH by adding lime in the late autumn. Conversely, if it is alkaline you will need to lower the pH by adding sulphur. If you have a garden with soil at the extremes of the pH balance the easiest solution is to make a raised bed for your herbs – it is not worth attempting to fight nature by trying to transform the pH balance of your entire garden.

Whilst adjustments in pH levels can be made, never add lime at the same time as compost, fertiliser or manure as a chemical reaction can destroy the effects of both processes. Lime is available from garden centres and hardware stores in the form of calcium carbonate or calcium hydroxide. The rate at which you will need to apply it will depend on the pH level of your soil; do a test and follow the instructions on the packet. Simple pH testing kits are readily available and simple to use. To decrease the soil's pH you will need to add sulphur. This is not usually added specifically as a fertiliser because soil reserves are replenished by recirculated organic matter. Nitrogen fertilisers in liquid form can also

be used to considerably reduce pH levels over a number of years; these are also widely available from garden centres.

Coping with weeds

A weed is actually just a plant growing in the wrong place – nettles and dandelions rank as herbs and the pernicious horsetail (*Equisetum arvense*) is in fact the oldest known herb. Any patch of ground used for growing herbs, however, will need to be cleared of weeds and then kept clean.

Digging is the time-honoured method of weed removal and when done thoroughly is highly effective. However, organic purists argue that digging more than once every five years is an entirely unnatural activity and one that disturbs the natural balance and structure of the soil – good news for those who hate wielding a spade! The theory is that worms do a better job of aerating the soil and distributing nutrients than any human can with a spade, and that applying mulches to the soil's surface is a far more efficient way of eradicating weeds and conditioning the soil than digging. This may be so, but it may initially be necessary to dig over a new herb bed to aerate the soil and to improve drainage by incorporating grit and sand.

Blanket mulches

The most efficient method of weed control is to apply mulch to the surface. Impenetrable blanket mulches suppress and smother weeds, but they do not provide a quick-fix solution to a weed problem as it can take a year or more to completely

clear a patch of weeds. One of the most effective forms of blanket mulch is a length of old carpet. It may look unsightly but it can save hours of laborious hand weeding. Blanket mulches are best applied in early spring, when weeds are just starting to grow.

Hand weeding

Clearing a patch of ground by hand is time-consuming and hard work, but it will allow you to plant up a herb bed much sooner than simply laying a blanket mulch would. It is worth taking some time over the process and doing a thorough job, as you will regret any haste later in the season. Try to remove every piece of root: every small piece of perennial root left in the soil can sprout a new plant and before you know it the problem has been exacerbated. Pernicious perennial weeds like bindweed (*Calystegia sepium*), couch grass (*Elymus repens*), creeping buttercup (*Ranunculus ficaria*), creeping thistle (*Cirsium arvense*), dandelion (*Taraxacum officinale*), dock (*Rumex*) and ground elder (*Aegopodium podagraria*) are the worst offenders. Be cautious about putting these weeds on to your compost heap; a seed or a tiny piece of root could survive the composting process where the heat has not built up sufficiently to kill it. Stinging nettles are a perennial nuisance but they do help make nutritious compost. Annuals like chickweed (*Stellaria media*), hairy bittercress (*Cardamine hirsuta*), groundsel (*Senecio vulgaris*) and shepherd's purse (*Capsella bursapastoris*) can also be problematic – always try to hoe or hand weed before these annuals set seed.

Feeding the soil

Many herbs will thrive in soil that is low in nutrients and will withstand healthy neglect, but a few, such as comfrey, coriander and angelica, demand a rich soil. In fact most plants benefit from the addition to the soil of some good compost or organic matter on an annual basis. Moreover some soils are hungrier than others; sandy soils in particular leach nutrients and require more frequent feeding and conditioning. Manure is readily available, but should be well rotted before it is incorporated into the soil. If you want to garden organically then check your sources very carefully, as manure is not necessarily organic.

Compost

Compost is the accelerated rotting down of green waste which, in time, is converted into a soil-like material. It is perfectly easy to make your own compost, but do take the time to understand the composting process – a successful compost heap is a world away from the pile of twigs and lawn cuttings that sits at the end of the garden for years doing nothing at all. It is much harder to make and work an effective compost heap without a bin – good insulation is part of the composting process. A well-insulated heap will start to heat up rapidly to temperatures exceeding 60°C (140°F). Indeed, a good compost heap will get so hot that it 'cooks', reaching temper-

atures high enough to kill weed seeds and destroy disease spores.

Compost bins

Compost bins need not be expensive; a range of styles is readily available from garden centres or they can be made at home easily and cheaply. Some local authorities actively promote the recycling of household waste with special offers on compost bins and water butts – check to see what is available in your area. Choose your bin carefully – the larger the bin the more heat your compost heap will generate. Ideally, you would have two or three bins together, each around 1m² (10 sq ft), to enable you to keep the process moving along: one heap you are building up with household waste and garden cuttings; one is 'cooking'; and one contains compost ready for use.

Do not keep adding fresh material to a heap that is in the process of rotting down. Bins should be well ventilated – good air circulation and drainage are essential – but require lids, or covers, to keep the rain out. Some bins can be turned on a pivot, which in theory takes the effort out of mixing or turning the heap over, but take care not to over fill them as they can become too heavy to rotate easily.

Saving waste

Garden and household waste are the principal ingredients of a good compost mix. Recycle garden clippings, avoiding those nasty pernicious weeds such as ground elder and bindweed and use suitable

household leftovers – almost any organic vegetable waste such as crushed egg shells, vegetable peelings, tea leaves, coffee grounds and shredded paper. Leave out anything that will attract vermin such as meat, fish, cheese or leftover cooked food. Do not use the compost to dispose of dog turds or cat litter. Leave weeds out to wither and dry on a path before adding them to your compost. Ensure a mix of one part nitrogen-rich, sappy green material such as grass clippings, to two parts carbon-rich material such as twigs, bark and paper, and make sure that the heap is not so tightly packed as to exclude air. Try to cut down in size or shred larger material in order to help accelerate the process of decomposition.

A compost heap should contain roughly equal measures of wet and dry materials – you may need to pour a little water over the top when mixing it up. Activators build up the numbers of bacteria that actually convert the rubbish to humus. Herbs like comfrey and chamomile are natural activators and the addition of a few leaves will help speed up the composting process.

Mix your compost around once a week until it is 'cooked'. Just take a minute or two to turn it over – it speeds up the process and helps ensure everything gets broken down. A shovelful, or two, of a neighbour's well-cooked compost can also help to activate your heap.

It can take between three and six months to turn waste into good compost, depending on the contents and the time of

topiary balls or pyramids

1 Use a circular wire template to guide your cut when shaping balls.

2 For straight-sided shapes, bamboo canes or plywood templates will guide your cut.

year. If you need a helping hand to begin with there is plenty of organic compost and manure available on the market.

Leaf-mould

Fallen leaves are a wonderful source of organic matter, but they should be composted separately in an open mesh bin, as they take longer to decompose. Alternatively, they can be collected in a black bag and stored out of the way to rot down. The process will take around a year to complete, but it will make a lovely rich, black fibrous material that is ideal for mixing into potting compost.

Food supplements

Most herbs will not require supplementary feeding in the garden as they enjoy poor soil and feeding can result in overly lush growth, which will merely attract pests and diseases. However, container plants may well require an extra feed. Fertilisers are rated according to their nitrogen (N), phosphorous (P) and potassium (K) content.

Nitrogen stimulates growth and leaves, phosphorous benefits the roots and potassium boosts disease resistance and fruiting. Choose the right supplement to suit your plants' particular requirements.

Deficiency in any one of these areas is indicated by poor growth and yellowing of the leaves; however, the commonest problems are caused by lack of nitrogen and potassium. Container plants in particular suffer from lack of nitrogen, which will result in spindly growth and pale foliage – perhaps spotted with yellow and pink patches. Fruiting plants are likely to be affected by shortages in potassium: leaves will discolour and brown, yellow and purple spots will appear in patches or on the leaf tip and margin.

Fertiliser comes in various forms, from pelleted chicken manure (check sources if you are gardening organically) to liquid herbal feeds you can make yourself, such as comfrey (*see below and page 166*), borage (*see below and page 74*) or stinging nettle (*see below and page 176*).

Comfrey fertiliser

Nitrogen-rich comfrey makes an excellent liquid fertiliser. First, you need to grow a reasonable amount of comfrey to have sufficient leaves for the job – around 6kg (14lb) for a 60litre (20gallon) water butt. These should be packed into a net bag – to avoid any need for sieving. Then they need to be crushed or bashed about a bit (good for relieving tension), weighed down with a brick in the butt, covered in water and left for several weeks. The result is very dark and smelly soup, which must be watered down to a pale yellow before use. The feed has a high potassium content and is excellent for feeding tomato plants.

Borage and nettle fertiliser

Both borage and nettle fertiliser can be made in the same way as for comfrey (*see above*); borage is rich in nitrogen and is useful for feeding brassicas (members of the cabbage family), while nettle fertiliser is purported to make plants more resistant to pests and diseases.

plaited bay

1 Select three strong, young green stems on a plant that is under 1.5m (5ft) and remove any other stems. Trim off any side shoots from the three remaining stems.

2 Plait or twist the stems loosely – remember that the stems will thicken as the plant matures – then stake for support. Allow the bushy crown to develop once the plaited stem has reached its desired final height.

Raised beds

Whilst herbs are extremely easy going plants, they will not tolerate waterlogged soil. Where this could be a problem, the easiest solution is to build a raised bed. These have the added advantage of looking attractive and being easier to work. They are relatively simple to build and can be made from stone, brick or timber. Recycled railway sleepers make construction very simple. Make raised beds 60–75cm (2–2½ft) high and fill the bottom third with coarse drainage (broken bricks and stone). Put a mix of soil and gravel in the middle third and top up with a mix of topsoil and compost.

Pruning

The fact that herbs are so easy and trouble free to grow is one of the pleasures of their cultivation. However, by the same principle, growth can rapidly run out of control if it is not checked. Shrubby herbs, such as lavender, santolina, bay and *Artemisia*, need regular pruning to keep

them in good shape. Cut off the flowering stems in late summer. In the spring cut the plant back into shape, but take care not to cut back too far. Always ensure you can see new shoots below the point at which you are pruning, as this way you can be confident that you are not cutting into old wood. If you cut into old wood the plant will not be able to produce any new shoots. Ideally, repeat this procedure every spring. If you leave it for a few years your beautiful shrub may be beyond help.

Containing spread

Mint is legendary for its ability to run riot in the garden and it is very hard to eradicate once it has spread. Growth is best controlled by planting it in a plastic pot, or by sinking a long pipe (minimum length 45cm/18in) into the flower bed and planting the mint inside it to curtail root spread. Other creeping plants such as sweet woodruff will need to have growth checked or they will quietly advance across the herb garden. The secret is to dig up any

unwanted plants before they have a chance to flower.

Tidying up

Skeletal plant remains may look aesthetic covered in frost, but it is not advisable to leave herbs to overwinter like this. Tall stems are buffeted by the winds, which can often destabilise a plant, leaving it vulnerable to frost. Many of the aromatic herbs like *Artemisia* work as natural insect repellents so after you have pruned them down, scatter the cuttings around the vegetable garden.

Topiary

Some herbs are good candidates for simple topiary shapes. Bay and box balls or standards are garden design classics, but increasingly plants like rosemary and lavender are now being trained into more formal designs.

It is very simple to train a plant into a standard shape, but you will need to be patient as it may take several years to

twisted bay

1 Select a young plant with a strong leader stem, cut away any other stems and trim back all side shoots.

2 Stake the plant with a stout post and train the stem around the post. Continue to strip away side shoots.

3 Allow the bushy crown to develop once the twisted stem has reached its desired height. It is possible to twist more than one stem around a post, but it will be harder to achieve a good finished effect.

reach its full glory. Grow your shrub of choice until it is 20cm (8in) over the desired finished height. Clip out the growing tip and then remove all the side shoots below the desired finished depth. Trim all remaining growth back to two or three leaves to encourage bushy new growth. Repeat this process each time the plant has grown shoots with another four to five leaves, trimming back to leave a fraction more each time. This cut-and-grow technique allows the plant to gradually thicken out until the ball shape is fully developed. Remember that proportions are important – the longer the stem length, the larger the ball shape should be. Once the standard is established it should require only a light pruning in early and late summer.

Plaited bay

To plait a bay, you need a young plant, no more than 1.5m (5ft) high. Select three young stems that are still slightly green. Plait them then stake them for support. Allow the plant to keep growing, stripping off any side shoots. When it has reached the desired height, allow the standard head to develop with the cut-and-grow technique described above. This will allow the plant to thicken and grow on a fraction at a time. It takes about ten years for a plaited bay to look fully mature.

Twisted bay

To train a twisted bay, stake a young plant with a 5cm (2in) diameter post. Select a strong, slightly green stem and wind it around the post, stripping off side shoots. Train it this way until it reaches the desired height then allow the standard head to develop with the cut-and-grow technique described above. It will take around 12–15 years before the stem can support itself without the stake. For a double twist follow the same procedure using two plants.

shaping a hedge
Run a line with sticks and string at the required cutting height to guide your shears. For a perfect shape cut a template from plywood and use this as your cutting guide.

Hedging

Hedges feature in all classic herb gardens. Whilst they are decorative, short hedges also allow the different species and varieties of herb to be segregated for easy identification and use. Taller hedges can screen more sensitive herbs from cruel winds and provide the kind of sheltered environment they enjoy. Plants such as yew, rosemary, box, lavender and santolina are classic favourites.

To grow a solid hedge, clip the sides regularly to encourage dense, bushy growth and always cut the hedge so that the base is a little wider than the top. Aesthetics aside, this protects the hedge from being damaged by heavy snowfalls. The key to the perfect clipped hedge is to run a line of string along the length, set to the desired height of cut, as a guide for your shears.

Herb lawns

When walked over, herb lawns release wonderful fragrance. The chamomile lawn is the best known: good, low-growing varieties to choose from include *Chamaemelum nobile* 'Flore Pleno' and 'Treneague'. Creeping thymes and Corsican or pennyroyal mints are equally suitable. Although a herb lawn will not need mowing it will require hand weeding, and establishing it will be much harder than for a grass lawn. A herb lawn should ideally have a layered foundation of 8cm (3in) hardcore, 8cm (3in) gravel and 15cm (6in) topsoil. Plant the herbs 10–15cm (4–6in) apart and keep off the area for at least 12 weeks. Herb lawns do not respond well to heavy use, so it is advisable to lay a path of stepping steps across to keep wear and tear to a minimum.

Clipped hedges

Plant	Spacing	Ultimate height	Frequency of cut
Box	30cm (12in)	30–60cm (1–2ft)	2–3 times in growing season
Lavender	30cm (12in)	60–100cm (2–3ft)	After flowering
Rosemary	45cm (18in)	1–2m (3–6ft)	After flowering
Santolina	30cm (12in)	60cm (2ft)	2–3 times in growing season
Yew	60cm (2ft)	1.2–6m (4–20ft)	Twice yearly in summer and autumn

Pests and Diseases

Useful companion plants

Borage (*Borago officinalis*)
Chamomile (*Chamaemelum nobile*)
Chives (*Allium schoenoprasum*)
Coneflower (*Echinea*)
Fennel (*Foeniculum vulgare*)
French marigold (*Tagetes*)
Garlic (*Allium sativum*)
Golden rod (*Solidago*)
Horseradish (*Armoracia rusticana*)
Hyssop (*Hyssopus officinalis*)
Nasturtium (*Tropaeolum majus*)
Southernwood (*Artemisia abrotanum*)
Sweet pea (*Lathyrus odoratus*)
Tansy (*Tanacetum vulgare*)
Thyme (*Thymus vulgaris*)
Wormwood (*Artemisia absinthium*)
Yarrow (*Achillea millefolium*)

In addition to their good looks and culinary attractions, herbs have the bonus of being naturally very resistant to most pests and diseases. What is more, the fragrance of many aromatic plants acts positively as an insect repellent, which is why they are often grown alongside vegetables. Useful companion plants particularly renowned for discouraging pests and diseases include nasturtiums, chives, garlic, thyme and hyssop, but there are many more. One herb in particular, pyrethrum, is a natural insecticide, and chamomile is believed to act as a general plant tonic, capable of restoring health and vigour to any ailing plants growing nearby.

It is the leafier herbs that can come under attack, and plants and seedlings grown in the artificial environment of a greenhouse are always more susceptible to attack by pests and diseases. Good gardening practices can do much to prevent problems occurring: clear away garden rubbish, pick off and destroy any diseased leaves as soon as they appear, and remove any visible pests. Avoid over watering all herbs, but particularly seedlings and young plants. If plants are well cultivated in good soil they will grow strong and healthy and will be able to withstand attack.

Given that herbs are so naturally resistant to pests and diseases, if they do come under attack it makes good sense to try to treat the problem using as few toxic chemicals as possible or, even better, none at all. This will be especially important for plants that you intend to use in cooking or to take internally as a home-made treatment for a minor ailment.

Barriers and traps

Some simple methods for outsmarting outdoor pests are extremely effective. Erecting a physical barrier to keep pests out of a specific area works well – nets, meshes, fleeces and plastic sheets can all be called into action for deterring rabbits, butterflies, carrot fly and birds but will probably really be needed only to protect salad crops. Different pests need different approaches. A popular method for discouraging slugs is to ring susceptible plants with a rough material such as eggshells, wood ash or sand. Another approach involves laying all manner of traps: orange halves and saucers full of beer, bran or milk will appeal to slugs; they can then be collected and disposed of. Straw-filled upturned flowerpots on sticks plunged into the ground attract sleepy earwigs, which can then be collected and destroyed.

Working with nature

The best way of controlling pests outdoors is to actively encourage natural predators into your garden – namely hoverflies, lady-birds, lacewings and assorted beetles. Planting plenty of open-centred flowers, such as those found on herbs like calendula, nasturtiums and poppies, will attract hoverflies into your garden. Building shelters made from hollow stems or planting some evergreen shrubs will give lacewings a winter refuge.

Biological control

Over the last 20 years, there have been huge advances in methods of biological pest control, which rely on introducing natural predators. For use in the greenhouse there are biological systems to help you control everything from vine weevil to red spider mite. Parasitic wasps have proved effective: *Encarsia formosa* will munch on whitefly, while *Aphidus* will consume aphids. The predatory mite *Phytoseilus* will digest the dreaded red spider mite and *Nematodes* will destroy the vine weevil grub. These systems are increasingly readily available commercially, usually by mail order. You simply order a batch of whichever predator will prey on the particular pest that is causing problems.

Most forms of predator control are suitable for use in confined areas rather than outside, but a few can be used successfully outdoors. *Phasmarhabditis*, for example, are parasites that live in the soil and kill slugs. Applied early in the season, they can be very effective in minimising slug damage.

Herbal insecticides

An insecticide made from pyrethrum (*Tanecetum cinerariifolium*), a hardy perennial that grows 30cm (12in) high, can be used against aphids and spider mites. It can also be used safely on the skin as an insect repellent and it can be sprinkled on all common insects that invade the house, including flies, ants, cockroaches and mosquitoes.

Pyrethrum has been used effectively as a natural insecticide for hundreds of years. It is native to Western Yugoslavia and Albania, but is now widely grown for commercial purposes. The active ingredi-

ent within the plant paralyses the nervous system of many insects, yet is non-toxic to mammals and environmentally friendly, so safe to use.

You can test out the deadly effect of this plant yourself by catching some flies under a glass and slipping in a few powdered dried flower heads – the flies should become groggy within a few minutes and die. The flowers will act as a fumigator when burnt.

Remedies for disease

Some fungal diseases can be combated with herb solutions if prompt action is taken. Chamomile flowers, for instance, are reputed to help prevent damping off disease, which is such a threat to seedlings. A handful of fresh flowers, or two tablespoons of dried ones, steeped in 1litre (1¾pints) of freshly boiled water for ten minutes is all that is required. Strain and spray over seedlings as soon as the mixture has cooled.

Horsetail (*Equisetum arvense*) can be helpful in combating root or fungus diseases. Make up a solution to the strength of just one part horsetail to 50 parts water – do not be tempted to make it any stronger as horsetail is a powerful herb. Boil the mix for 15 minutes then allow it to cool. The day before applying, make sure that the ground around the affected plant is well watered, whether by rain or manually; do not use the solution on very dry soil. Pour the horsetail solution around the base of the affected plant, rather than on the foliage.

Planning a Herb Garden

Herbs for a culinary garden

Angelica (*Angelica archangelica*)
Basil (*Ocimum basilicum*)
Bay (*Laurus nobilis*)
Chervil (*Anthriscus cerefolium*)
Chives (*Allium schoenoprasum*)
Coriander (*Coriandrum sativum*)
Dill (*Anethum graveolens*)
Fennel (*Foeniculum vulgare*)
Garlic (*Allium sativum*)
Lemon thyme (*Thymus x citriodorus*)
Lovage (*Levisticum officinale*)
Mint (*Mentha*)
Oregano (*Origanum vulgare*)
Parsley (*Petroselinum crispum*)
Rosemary (*Rosmarinus officinalis*)
Sage (*Salvia officinalis*)
Sweet cicely (*Myrrhis odorata*)
Sweet marjoram (*Origanum majorana*)
Tarragon (*Artemisia dracunculus*)
Thyme (*Thymus vulgaris*)
Winter savory (*Satureja montana*)

Herb plants can be readily incorporated into an existing garden scheme or they can be grown in a dedicated garden, the design for which can range from the minimal to the magnificent. Whether you plan a traditional knot garden or simply to use an army of brightly painted containers, the key to success is realism. So start by planting herbs that you know you will use – the most beautiful herb garden can be deemed a failure if its leaves, flowers, fruits, roots and berries are never harvested or its perfumes enjoyed.

A good starting point is to draw up a list of all the herbs that you already use, whether you buy them fresh or dried. If you begin with these plants you can more or less guarantee that you will soon establish a successful working herb garden. From here you can begin to expand your list to include the culinary classics as well as herbs that you use in teas or for treating minor family ailments. Start experimenting with unfamiliar herbs. Culinary herbs are subject to fashion trends and the fact that they have fallen out of favour does not mean they taste anything other than fabulous. It is worth noting, for instance, that a growing guide to salads published in the seventeenth century included such contemporary favourites as chicory, endive, sorrel, rocket, fennel and purslane, all of which later fell out of regular use in Britain.

Situation

Herbs are remarkably tolerant, disease resistant and easy to grow. Nevertheless, to be really productive it is imperative that they are planted in the right position for their requirements.

What you want to grow and what you can grow in reality will be determined to some degree by the environment For instance, many popular herbs are indigenous to the Mediterranean region and so require plenty of sunshine. So whether you are preparing a completely new herb garden, planting up a few pots or dotting selected herbs around the flower border, you will always need to be aware of the needs of your chosen plants. A herb that is described as enjoying a sunny situation will, weather permitting, require approximately seven hours of sunshine daily. It will like warmth and will particularly enjoy close proximity to stone, brick and gravel, which bounce the heat back at them. A herb that is described as enjoying semi-shade will thrive on around four hours of sunshine a day.

Access

Assess your garden carefully in order to decide where you can best position a herb bed or create a dedicated herb garden. Ideally, it will be close to the kitchen and easily accessible. Ensure that there is year-round access to your herbs – if you have to wade through a sea of mud, for instance, to pick a sprig of rosemary in the middle of winter you probably will not bother to venture out.

Separate beds

Whilst many herbs, such as lavender, fare well in a mixed flower border, others are best cultivated in their own space. Traditionally herbs were laid out in a series of small beds, a practice that is efficient because it effectively separates different species allowing for speedy identification. And if one thing is important when using herbs, it is the ability to identify them confidently. The divisions can also form pleasing patterns.

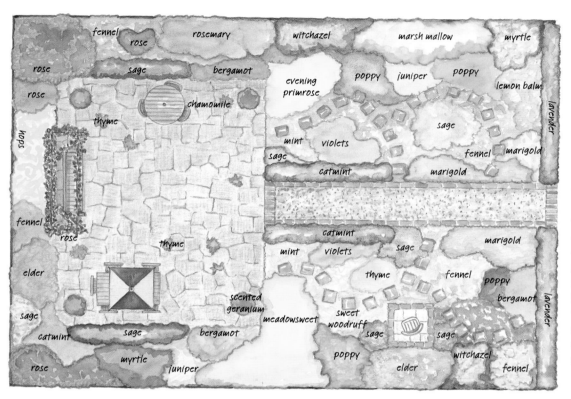

In the garden plan (labels as shown):
fennel, rose, rosemary, witchazel, marsh mallow, myrtle, rose, sage, bergamot, evening primrose, poppy, juniper, poppy, lemon balm, rose, chamomile, thyme, lavender, hops, mint, violets, sage, sage, fennel, marigold, catmint, marigold, fennel, catmint, marigold, rose, thyme, mint, violets, sage, thyme, fennel, poppy, elder, bergamot, lavender, sage, scented geranium, meadowsweet, sweet woodruff, sage, sage, catmint, sage, bergamot, poppy, witchazel, myrtle, juniper, elder, fennel, rose

Making a plan

Before you make a decision about the design for a new herb garden it is a good idea to make a plan. Measure out the space you have available, using a long tape measure. Transfer the dimensions to graph paper so that you can make a scale drawing. Note the aspect of the site then try out different repeat patterns until you have a design that you are pleased with. Mark out the finished design in the garden using canes or pegs and string. To work a herb bed comfortably you should be able to reach its centre easily from the edge; therefore beds should be no wider than 1.5–1.8m (5–6ft). Paths should be no less than 75cm (2½ft) wide, and a path of 1.1m (3½ft) width will comfortably accommodate a wheelbarrow. Remember that in addition to laying paths you must think about the cultivation of the herb beds and check drainage and soil type (*see page 21*). Always complete any hard land-scaping work before you start cultivating the herb beds.

Knot gardens

A traditional knot garden features low clipped hedges of box, lavender or san-tolina in a series of repeat patterns – tra-ditionally the lovers knot. The hedges form the divisions between the different species of herbs and maintain a crisp sense of order within which the herbs are allowed to run riot. The herbs are planted in repeat sequences so that the same planting scheme is reflected throughout, creating a mirror image of plant colours and heights. Knot gardens require great discipline in cultivation, planting and maintenance but they are incredibly pleasing to the eye.

The culinary herb garden

The flavour and quality of freshly picked, home-grown herbs are unassailable. Most culinary herbs are really very easy to culti-vate and once you have grown your own you will never look back. A culinary herb garden should include the basic ingredi-ents of the three famous herb mixes:

enclosed herb garden

The key to creating a successful perfumed garden is to ensure that it is enclosed so that fragrances hang in the air. Fencing, hedging and trellis will all act as windbreaks to varying degrees. This should be a secluded and relaxing spot, so separate it from the house or the rest of the garden with a path through the plants that leads to a com-fortable seating area. Most herbs are fragrant, choose your favourites and remember to get a good mix of heights, for example climbing roses, bushy clouds of fennel and low-growing clumps of thyme. Aim for a relaxed, airy informal planting scheme. Brush against plants as you walk and place low-growing herbs in the path and on the terrace so that a heady mix of aromas is released. Use pots for sweetly scented seasonal plantings such as hyacinths, wallflowers and lilies.

Herbs for an enclosed garden

Apothecary's rose (*Rosa gallica*)
Bergamot (*Monarda didyma*)
Chamomile (*Chamaemelum nobile*)
Eau de cologne mint (*Mentha x piperita* f. *citrata*)
Evening primrose (*Oenothera biennis*)
Lavender (*Lavandula*)
Lemon balm (*Melissa officinalis*)
Lemon thyme (*Thymus x citriodorus*)
Myrtle (*Myrtus communis*)
Peppermint (*Mentha x piperita*)
Rosemary (*Rosmarinus officinalis*)
Sage (*Salvia*)
Sweet violet (*Viola odorata*)

functional herb garden

This garden is designed to be easy to plant and use, and it makes plant identification very straightforward as each species is separated off from the next. The dividers can be as simple as shells and pebbles, or you can sink in pieces of wood, brick or stone as required. Surround plant beds with paths for comfortable year-round access. Raised beds allow you to control planting conditions and make the area very user friendly. Leave gaps in the path for planting low-growing sweet-smelling herbs such as chamomile and thyme, which will release fragrance when you brush them as you walk by.

Herbs for a tea garden
Anise hyssop (*Agastache anethiodora*)
Apothecary's rose (*Rosa gallica*)
Bergamot (*Monarda didyma*)
Curly mint (*Mentha spicata*)
Dog rose (*Rosa canina*)
Fennel (*Foeniculum vulgare*)
German chamomile (*Chamaemelum recutita*)
Lemon balm (*Melissa officinalis*)
Rosemary (*Rosmarinus officinalis*)
Sage (*Salvia officinalis*)
Thyme (*Thymus vulgaris*)

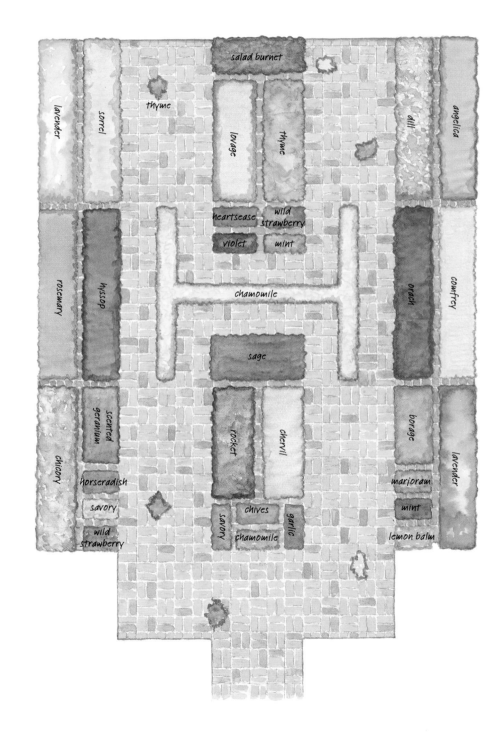

bouquet garni – bay, thyme and parsley (see page 172); fines herbes – chervil, chives, parsley and tarragon (see page 138); and herbes de Provence – rosemary and thyme combined with basil, marjoram, savory and tarragon. Other essentials include chives, mint and garlic, which are commonly required in the kitchen. If you are short of space all of these herbs can be grown in containers, so do not let the lack of a garden prevent you from growing your own herbs.

The perfumed garden

By nature herbs tend to be intensely aromatic plants and the diverse range of fragrances can combine together to make a most pleasurable and sensual garden. When planning a perfumed garden, create a space that is sheltered from prevailing winds so that scent can hang in the air. Plant hedges of rosemary, lavender and bay, erect willow hurdles or make a post or trellis screen over which to grow roses, honeysuckle and jasmine. Run paths through the area so that you will brush against the plants as you pass. Grow chamomile and creeping thymes in the paths so that your feet release fresh injections of perfume into the air. Include a seat so that you can sit and breathe deeply as you enjoy the most natural form of aromatherapy.

A tea garden

Fresh herb teas bear about as much resemblance to commercial herb teas as fresh herbs do to dried and I cannot recommend them highly enough. If you want a completely new taste experience make your own tea, or infusion, from fresh herbs. The process is simple: take a few sprigs of your chosen herb, pour on boiling water, leave for a few minutes, strain and drink. Stir in some honey if you need to sweeten the tea.

Many herbs make pleasant and useful teas. The early Americans commonly used bergamot as a tea substitute during the War of Independence, when traditional supplies were cut. Fennel, anise hyssop and young mint leaves all make digestive teas. Chamomile tea is known to be soothing and sedative and rose-petal tea has long been regarded as a most refined afternoon beverage. Rosemary tea, sweetened with a little honey, is my preferred drink of choice.

Not all herb teas can be drunk with impunity, however. Any substance taken to excess can be toxic and herbs are no exception. Sage tea, another of my favourites, is a case in point. It should be consumed for short periods of time only as it can be toxic if taken to excess and can damage the central nervous system. The occasional cup, though, is a real treat. Some herbs are unsuitable for use by pregnant women or anyone suffering from a kidney problem. Check the Herb Directory (see page 50) or consult a herbalist before trying a new tea. It is always worth taking the time and trouble to double-check to ensure safety – you will quickly learn what you can take with impunity and what you cannot.

Medicinal garden

Herbs rank as the most powerful and potent plants in horticulture. Alternative therapies such as homeopathy and herbalism have long recognised the value of herbs, but it is only recently that scientists have undertaken serious research into the properties of some of these plants and investigated the scientific basis behind the success of traditional 'old wives' remedies'.

Herbs can be safely used to treat many minor complaints, just as your great grandmother would have done generations ago without a moment's thought. Bruises and sprains would have been eased with compresses, and an upset stomach soothed with chamomile tea. These herbal remedies are still valid and many provide very gentle treatment that is particularly useful for small children who will always prefer the gentle calming of a cold compress to a stinging proprietary antiseptic cream.

Nonetheless, herbs must always be treated with respect. Never attempt to treat anything other than minor complaints without the guidance of a qualified herbalist and, if you are in any doubt at all, seek the advice of a qualified physician. Plants are not produced in controlled conditions and one herb in one garden may be more potent than the same plant growing next door. Remember, too, that it is important that you use only the cited species of medicinal plants – exotic cultivars and varieties will not have the same properties.

Herbs for a medicinal garden

Chamomile (*Chamaemelum nobile*)
Comfrey (*Symphytum officinale*)
Dill (*Anethum graveolens*)
Fennel (*Foeniculum vulgare*)
Feverfew (*Tanacetum parthenium*)
Garlic (*Allium sativum*)
Horseradish (*Armoracia rusticana*)
Juniper (*Juniperus officinalis*)
Lavender (*Lavandula*)
Lemon balm (*Melissa officinalis*)
Marigold (*Calendula officinalis*)
Marsh mallow (*Althaea officinalis*)
Meadowsweet (*Filipendula ulmaria*)
Rosemary (*Rosmarinus officinalis*)
Sage (*Salvia officinalis*)
Thyme (*Thymus*)

formal herb garden

Although it requires some discipline in planning and maintenance, this garden is very pleasing to the eye. Plan the layout carefully so that it accommodates all your requirements from the start and make a focal point at the centre of your scheme – anything from a handsome pot to a water feature. Formal hedging of box, lavender or santolina should contain the beds, or use bushy herbaceous perennials such as catmint. Beds should be planted up with an element of repetitive planting, but it can be sufficient to mark the centre point of each bed with a structural planting such as a piece of topiary or a standard weeping rosebush.

Container gardens

The great thing about herbs is that they make first-class container plants so lack of space need never curb your enthusiasm or restrict your home-grown supply. The many species that enjoy well-drained soil, hate getting their roots too wet and love plenty of heat are naturally adapted to container living. Indeed, the most frequently used herbs are often those that are grown in handy containers outside the back door or on the kitchen windowsill. There are no rules about what type of container to use for herbs, so let your imagination run riot; beautiful terracotta urns for formal gardens, or contemporary aluminium designs for the more modern approach. Plastic or fibreglass pots can always be personalised with a lick of paint. Even the humble tin can, with holes punctured in its base, will make an effective container.

Try to use the largest containers your space will possibly permit; minimum sizes should be 25x25cm (10x10in). It is always worth following this advice, as plants really do grow much better in larger containers. Always ensure that you have good drainage at the bottom of the pot by placing some crocks or gravel over the base. If you are worried about soil leaching through the base, use a piece of sacking or muslin as a barrier. You can experiment with gravel, stones, shells, glass beads or china fragments as decorative mulch — it will prevent the sun from baking the surface of the soil, discourage weeds as well as looking good.

Hanging baskets

Some herbs will grow quite contentedly in a hanging basket for a season, but since most dislike wind always try to make sure they are located in a sheltered spot. Chamomile, thyme, prostrate rosemary and nasturtiums are quite tolerant of basket conditions. To help prevent moisture loss, you need to line the basket with a layer of plastic with holes punched through to allow free drainage. If you want to disguise the plastic, line the basket first with a more attractive organic material. Sphagnum moss is the traditional choice, but a more environmentally friendly alternative would be anything from an old woolly jumper, through hay and compressed paper, to cocoa moss or a cocoa-fibre liner. Half-fill the basket with suitable compost, place trailing herbs around the edge then fill in the gaps with taller plants. Fill around the plants with more compost and firm gently.

Potting composts for containers and baskets

There are plenty of potting composts suitable for container gardening on sale, but it is perfectly possible and well worth trying to make your own, although it does require some care. A growing medium must be water retentive and well aerated, with a structure that can withstand heavy watering. It consists of two main components: bulky material to hold the plants upright and nutrients to feed them. A good blend for growing herbs in containers is four parts good-quality weed-free garden soil, three parts well-rotted garden compost and two parts grit or sharp sand.

Different mixes suit different plant requirements. Use well-rotted leaf-mould alone or a mix of garden soil and leaf-mould for seed sowing. Mix up three parts garden soil to one part manure and one part leaf-mould for greedy, fast-growing plants such as rocket and basil. Nutrient-rich worm compost is ideal for hungry hanging baskets or for giving containers a boost.

All containers need a little annual maintenance. Many plants benefit from being lifted and divided, allowing you to refresh the compost and increase your stock. They may require top-dressing — replacing the top layer of the soil with new compost and slow-release fertiliser — or they may need to be moved to a larger pot if they become root bound.

Herbs for containers

Basil (*Ocimum basilicum*)
Bay (*Laurus nobilis*)
Catmint (*Nepeta cataria*)
Chives (*Allium schoenoprasum*)
Feverfew (*Tanacetum parthenium*)
Hyssop (*Hyssopus officinalis*)
Lavender (*Lavandula*)
Lemon balm (*Melissa officinalis*)
Marigold (*Calendula officinalis*)
Mint (*Mentha*)
Nasturtium (*Tropaeolum majus*)
Oregano (*Origanum vulgare*)
Parsley (*Petroselinum crispum*)
Rosemary (*Rosmarinus*)
Sage (*Salvia officinalis*)
Sweet marjoram (*Origanum majorana*)
Tarragon (*Artemisia dracunculus*)
Thyme (*Thymus vulgaris*)
Wild strawberry (*Fragaria vesca*)

using herbs

Harvesting and Storing Herbs

Anyone who is interested in using herbs as part of their everyday life, be it for cooking, making teas and home remedies or using around the home, will want to use the best produce they can find. This usually means growing the herbs at home. However, knowing when to harvest, even the best time of the day to pick, and how to store your crop will ensure that you always get the maximum benefit from your plants.

Even if you prefer to use your herbs fresh rather than dried, the natural cycle of most plants will mean that there are times of the year when parts are no longer useful or even available. The real skill in utilising herbs is to ensure that, whenever possible, you have a year-round supply. Many herbs respond well to home freezing or drying and, fortunately, the processes are relatively simple.

Harvesting

Different herbs reach their prime at different times, so if you are harvesting for drying, check the Herb Directory for the ideal time to pick them. Discard leaves and flowers that look withered or diseased or which have been attacked by insects.

Picking leaves

The flavour of all leaf herbs is best before the plant commences flowering so for drying you need to pick leaves before this occurs. You can continue to use fresh leaves for as long as your taste buds find the flavour palatable. However, even with evergreen herbs, such as bay, thyme, rosemary and sage, which can be picked throughout the year, the flavour is always superior prior to flowering.

The youngest and freshest leaves are always the sweetest flavoured and most succulent; older leaves can become bitter and overly strong in flavour. As a general rule it is best to collect leaves in the morning after all the dew has evaporated as this is when the essential oils in the leaves are at their most potent. Try to select clean leaves so that you do not have to wash them as this would defeat the purpose of picking them dry. If necessary, however, they can be carefully wiped to remove any dust or dirt. Always handle leaves gently.

Gathering flowers

Gather flowers when they are fully open, usually at midday on a fine sunny day. Treat them very gently. If you are unable to begin the drying process immediately put them in a cool room for a short period as they deteriorate rapidly in heat.

Collecting seed

Timing is all important when harvesting seed. Gathered too early, it will be green and likely to deteriorate, but if gathered late, it may have already dispersed before you get to it. Seed is generally ripe when it has turned from green to beige, brown or black in colour. Seed pods should feel very dry to the touch. Some seeds can be gathered directly from the plant simply by shaking the seed heads into a paper bag.

Digging up roots

Herb roots are most potent in autumn, after the plants have died back. Dig up annuals at the end of their first year, but allow perennial roots to mature for two to three years before harvesting. Clean roots thoroughly, removing any fibrous parts.

Cleaning bark

Make sure that bark is clean and free of insects. Wash it if necessary.

Storing fresh herbs

Fresh herbs tend to wilt very quickly once they have been picked. If you are not going to use them immediately, they are best stored in a plastic bag in the salad compartment or the door of the fridge until required. If freshly cut herbs start to wilt

decorative ice cubes

Certain flowers and leaves make very pretty ice cubes for use in summer fruit drinks and punches. Borage flowers and individual mint leaves are particularly attractive. Simply place a flower or leaf into each compartment of an ice tray, pour in the water and freeze.

very quickly before you can use them, put them in a plastic bag and revive them in the fridge.

Freezing herbs

For many culinary herbs, freezing is the best long-term storage method and is appealing because of its simplicity. We should no more think twice about freezing herbs than we do the glut of soft fruit in the summer. After all, what could be easier than freezing standard measures of parsley, dill, basil, chives, fennel, chervil, tarragon or sweet cicely for use later on? All you have to do is to put the clean herb in a plastic bag or a foil envelope and label it. Prepare each herb as if you were about to use it: remove leaves from stems and discard flowers, seeds and damaged leaves. Avoid putting huge quantities in a bag just because you have plenty, as it is harder to gauge quantities of a herb when it is frozen. Instead, freeze amounts that you would normally use in a single dish. You can also freeze portions of herb mixes such as *fines herbes* or *bouquet garni*.

Herb cubes

Chopped herbs can be stored in ice cube form. Simply place one tablespoon of the chopped herb in each cell of a good-sized cube tray, pour on water and freeze. If your recipe requires the herbs without any water, simply place the ice cube in a sieve to defrost. Some cooks argue that frozen herbs retain a little more of their flavour if the leaf is frozen intact and is chopped after defrosting.

Dried herbs

Part of the joy of using good culinary herbs is that they are seasonal and therefore one flavour follows another as the year progresses. However, some, especially the culinary classics like bay, marjoram, mint, oregano, rosemary, sage, savory and thyme, will be needed all year round. One of the secrets of successful drying is not to attempt to preserve every herb in the garden so choose carefully which herbs you want to preserve this way. When using dried herbs in cooking, remember that they are three to four times stronger in flavour than fresh herbs so adjust the amounts you use accordingly.

Drying herbs is not difficult, but if the concept invokes quaint images of picturesque bunches suspended from aged kitchen beams think again. This may look charming, but the herbs will dry coated in dust and cooking fumes. Herbs are best dried in a warm and airy room and should be kept out of direct sunlight – a shady corner is ideal. The drying process cannot be rushed for hurried drying will cause the essential oils to be lost. Begin the drying process as soon as possible after harvesting a plant, however. Herbs deteriorate rapidly after cutting and the longer a plant is left before drying the less effective the dried herb will be.

Dried herbs do not have an indefinite shelf life and should be stored for up to six months only, after which time their flavour fades. Fortunately, by the time they begin to deteriorate you will have cultivated a fresh supply to work with. Put unused dried herbs on the compost heap to rot down or around your vegetable or herb garden where they may still deter pests.

Equipment for drying

Different herbs may require different equipment for drying. Some can be laid on racks, which consist of muslin or cheesecloth stretched taut over a frame and stapled or tacked in place. Brown paper sheets, punctured with holes and secured to a frame with masking tape, can be used instead. Always prepare drying racks and paper prior to harvesting. Paper bags, string and tissue paper or newspaper can also be called for.

Evergreen, or semi-evergreen herbs, such as lavender, rosemary, sage, bay and thyme, can be dried in small bunches hung head down. Tie the stems together with string, cotton or twine, but do not use more than about eight stems in a bunch or the air will not circulate freely enough to allow them to dry fully. Ideally, hang them up somewhere dark and dust-free to dry, but you can cover the bunches with paper bags to keep them clean.

Small, feathery-leafed herbs, such as chervil and fennel, are best dried as leafy stalks and the leaves removed after the drying process is complete. Herbs with larger leaves, such as mint and sage, need to have the foliage stripped off prior to drying so that the leaves can be spread out over a frame to dry.

Flowers need to be laid out carefully on a muslin-covered frame so that they can hold their shape.

Microwave ovens

It is possible to dry herbs in a microwave oven, but predicting accurate drying times can be tricky – there is such a variation in oven temperatures that it is a case of trial and error. Some herbs can ignite if dried this way, so monitor the drying process carefully if you try this method!

Leaves and flowers

Leaves and flowers need to be dried in a warm, dark but well-ventilated environment, such as an airing cupboard or a loft. However, the drying process depends on plenty of dry fresh air rather than on heat, so artificial warmth is not essential. If you are in a position to be able to control room temperature, then for the first 24 hours a drying temperature of 32ºC (90ºF) is desirable, after which the level can be reduced to 24–26ºC (75–79ºF). At these temperatures many leaves will dry in four to seven days, but thicker leaves may take a little longer. If precise temperature control is not possible, the drying process may take up to a fortnight. When fully dried, leaves will feel dry and brittle; if they turn to powder they have been over dried. Flowers take a little longer than leaves to dry – from one to three weeks.

To store leaves and flowers, discard any hard stalks, and place them in a dark glass jar with an airtight lid, away from direct sunlight.

Seed

Artificial heat is not usually required to assist the drying process for seeds. To collect seeds, suspend flower heads upside down with a tray underneath to catch them as they drop out. Alternatively, you can tie a paper bag over the suspended flower heads. Either way, seeds will dry very quickly in an airy room, usually within a fortnight. If you dry seeds for household use, store them in an airtight container, but for propagation purposes store them in a cool dark environment.

Berries and fruit

Berries and fruit will benefit from being placed in an airing cupboard to accelerate the drying process. Turn plump fruit frequently to ensure even drying.

Roots

Roots should be thoroughly washed prior to drying and any top growth, hairs or fibrous offshoots removed. Most roots benefit from being roughly chopped to facilitate the drying process. Split large roots through the middle then cut into smaller pieces. They can be dried successfully in an oven set at 50–60ºC (30-40ºC if fan-assisted), but should be turned to ensure even drying. When fully dried, roots should break easily. Store them in airtight jars; if they later deteriorate and become soft discard them – they must not be used.

Bark

Leave bark to dry in a dark, warm and airy place. Drying time varies considerably according to the thickness of the bark. When fully dried store in an airtight jar.

Herbs in the Kitchen

making herb vinegar

A good-quality white or red wine vinegar is the best for making most herb vinegars. Most fresh herbs can be used as a flavouring (never use dried ones).

Chop enough fresh herbs to half-fill a bottle. Warm double their volume of wine vinegar and pour it over the herbs. Cover tightly and leave in a cool, dry place for about six weeks.

Strain the vinegar through a piece of muslin. Taste and add more vinegar if the flavour is too strong. Pour into sterilised glass bottles and seal with air-tight, corrosion-proof tops. Use within six months.

making herb oil

Herb oils can be brushed over meat and fish before grilling. To make a herb oil, choose a bland base oil such as sunflower, groundnut or safflower oil, or a mild olive oil.

Most culinary herbs are suitable. Choose from rosemary, thyme, tarragon, marjoram, fennel, savory, sage and basil. They should all be used fresh. Lightly bruise enough herb sprigs to half-fill a wide-necked glass bottle or jar. Cover the herbs with oil and seal with a corrosion-proof top.

Leave the oil for two weeks in a cool, dark place. Shake once a day.

Strain the oil, pressing down hard on the herbs. Taste. If the flavour is not strong enough, repeat the process. When the oil is ready, decant it into a sterilised dark glass bottle and seal with a corrosion-proof top. Use within six months.

Using herbs to flavour oil, vinegar and preserves, such as chutneys and jellies, is another way of extending their life. Preserving herbs in oil or vinegar for culinary use is a habit that has fallen out of practice. Yet it is a very effective way of harnessing the flavours and fragrance of fresh herbs and making them instantly accessible. In culinary terms it is an efficient, labour-saving device, providing a herb supply on tap and ready to use in an instant. These home-made preserves are fantastically impressive to visitors – they look pretty on the shelves, hint at natural culinary skills and make great presents!

Syrups and cordials are another way of capturing herb flavours. They can be used in summer drinks and many desserts. Flowers, too, can be held, albeit briefly, in suspended animation for use as pretty decoration for desserts and cakes.

On a much shorter time scale, fresh herbs can be used to flavour butter, which is delicious spread on bread and used in cooking. Similarly, herb butters can be used to add an extra dimension to simple fruit sauces, such as apple, which can also be frozen for convenient use at a later time.

Herb vinegar

Adding a herb to vinegar is a very simple and effective way to preserve its flavour, and in years past kitchens were packed with herb vinegars. Tarragon vinegar was tossed into salads, while horseradish vinegar was used to dress cold meat. Sweet vinegars made from fruit or flowers were also prized. Aromatic herbs such as basil, chervil, dill, garlic, marjoram, mint, rosemary, savory, tarragon and thyme all make delicious herb vinegar. They can be used individually or several can be combined, as in *fines herbes* vinegar.

Most herb vinegar is prepared by mixing about ten tablespoons of a gently pounded herb with 500ml (18fl oz) white wine or cider vinegar, and is ready for use after six weeks. The powerful flavour of malt vinegar is unsuitable. The vinegar should be added to the herb gradually, and some cooks advocate that it should be slightly warmed in a pan first. Before sealing the bottle, add a sprig of fresh herb for both identification and decoration.

The seeds of dill, fennel and coriander also make delicious vinegar but mix these in the proportions of two tablespoons lightly crushed seed to 600ml (1pint) vinegar.

Herb oil

A selection of herb oils is invaluable in the kitchen, but it is best to choose herbs that you use regularly. Basil, garlic and *bouquet garni* oil are commonly used herb oils. Basil oil harnesses the distinctive flavour of this popular herb very successfully and is excellent for Mediterranean dishes and for sprinkling over home-cooked pizza and pasta. Garlic is so widely used in cooking that a home-made garlic oil can be a real life saver whenever you are pressed for time; it will enable you to produce tasty salad dressings, stir-fries and pasta dishes in just a few moments. Similarly, *bouquet garni* oil can be convenient for cooking meats and stews.

Herb oil is usually prepared by mixing four tablespoons of a lightly pounded herb with 450ml (¾pint) olive oil, and is ready to use after two weeks. Before sealing the bottle, add a sprig of fresh herb for identification and as decoration. As herb oil will go rancid after about six months, it is unwise to make larger quantities than you can expect to use within that time, unless you want to give bottles away as gifts.

parsley butter (maître d'hôtel)

125g (4oz) butter, softened
2tbsp freshly chopped parsley
Lemon juice, to taste
Pinch of cayenne pepper

1 Cream the butter until soft. Add the parsley, lemon juice, cayenne and a pinch of salt and beat together. Shape the butter into a roll and wrap it in greaseproof paper or kitchen foil. Chill in the fridge.

2 To serve, cut into rounds about 5mm (¼in) thick. Serve with grilled white fish, steak or egg dishes.

Herb butter

Everyone is familiar with garlic bread, but many other herbs can be mixed with butter and used in a similar way. You can serve herb butter in hot bread or on toast, brush it on to steaks and fish prior to grilling or melt it over cooked vegetables. To make herb butter simply cream the butter and mix with a finely chopped herb – anything from mint to dill, horseradish or sage.

Preserves

While supermarkets offer a small selection of herb oils and vinegars there is little in the way of herb preserves and this is a great shame. Herb preserves offer bites of flavour that range from sharp through intense to perfect subtle sweetness. Home cooking comes into its own here and for a little effort it is possible to produce delicious sweet and savoury preserves.

Herb chutney and pickle

The addition of herbs to any basic chutney or pickle mix will give it an extra dimension that can transform simple fare like basic bread and cheese or a slice of cold meat. Mint and coriander are the best known types of chutney and making them is a relatively straightforward process.

Herb jelly

The visual perfection and clarity of taste of a jelly preserve are widely appealing, and a herb jelly, in essence an apple jelly flavoured with herbs, will make a delicious accompaniment to many meat and fish dishes. Home-made mint jelly, for instance, a traditional companion to lamb, has much more bite and taste than a commercially produced version. Sweet marjoram, rosemary, sage, tarragon, thyme and lemon thyme are all excellent flavourings for herb jellies.

The procedure (*see recipe opposite*) is much the same for both sweet and savoury jellies, but for sweet jellies substitute 150ml (¼pint) water for the vinegar and lemon juice used in savoury jellies. If you like delicate, perfumed flavours then sweet herb jellies are quite unique; try using lavender, lemon verbena, lemon balm, mint and rose. You can use ordinary cooking apples or crab apples for the jelly. If you use the latter, it is not worth bothering to core them as they are so small.

Herb apple sauces

A basic apple sauce is a delicious accompaniment for meat, especially pork, but it can be spiced up with the addition of herbs. Adding a few sage leaves (around four or five to two large cooking apples), for instance, transforms the flavour, and stirring in a spoonful of honey makes it even more appealing to anyone with a sweet tooth. Herb apple sauce can be frozen for use as required.

Flower syrups

Summer drinks, fruit salads, sorbets and ice cream can all be flavoured by the addition of a flower syrup. Syrups can be a bit of a fuss to make, but are uniquely delicious. They have been enjoyed for centuries, as the following recipe from *The Good Housewife's Handmaid*, 1585, attests. The method demands huge quantities of flower petals and a large reserve of patience. It requires the steeping of 450g (1lb) rose petals or violets in 1.7 litres (3pints) warm water in an earthenware container for eight hours, after which the mixture is strained and reheated and another 450g (1lb) of rose petals or violets added. The whole process has to be performed five times in total, after which the strained mixture needs to be measured and 450g (1lb) of sugar added for every 600ml (1pint) of liquid. Finally, the liquid is heated very gently until the sugar is completely dissolved.

Fortunately, there are easier ways of making cordials.

Crystallised flowers

As impressive decorations for cakes and desserts, crystallised flowers are hard to beat. They are easy to make and children love to help. Borage, primrose and violet flowers are the easiest to crystallise. They will last only a day or two, so ideally make them the day before they are required.

To crystallise the flowers, first add a pinch of salt to an egg white and beat it lightly without it becoming frothy. Dip freshly picked flowers into the egg white then into a dish of caster sugar and put them on a wire baking tray covered with greaseproof paper. Cover the flowers with another sheet of greaseproof paper and put the tray in a low oven with the door ajar, or in the airing cupboard, until dry. Store the flowers in an airtight container.

herb jelly

Makes 1.4kg (3lb)

2.3kg (5lb) cooking apples

Few sprigs of chosen fresh herb

1.1litres (2pints) distilled vinegar

Sugar

6–8tbsp freshly chopped mint,
    parsley or thyme; or
    6tbsp freshly chopped sage; or
    4tbsp freshly chopped rosemary

1 Remove any bruised or damaged
parts from the apples. Roughly chop
them without peeling or coring.

2 Put them into a large saucepan with
1.1litres (2pints) water and the herb
sprigs. Bring to the boil and simmer
gently for 4–5min or until soft and
pulpy, stirring from time to time to
prevent sticking. Add the vinegar
and boil for 5min.

3 Spoon the apple pulp into a jelly bag
and leave it to strain into a large bowl
for at least 12hr.

4 Discard the pulp. Measure the liquid
and put it into a preserving pan with
450g (1lb) sugar for each 600ml
(1pint) liquid. Heat gently, stirring,
until the sugar has dissolved. Boil
rapidly for 10min.

5 To test for setting, put a spoonful on
a chilled saucer; the jelly should wrinkle
when a finger is pulled through. When
the setting point is reached, take the
pan from the heat and remove any
scum with a slotted spoon. Stir in the
chopped herbs.

6 Cool slightly. Stir again to distribute
the herb then pot the jelly in warmed
sterilised jam jars and cover (*see page
145*). Use within six months.

Medicinal and Cosmetic Use

Apart from their culinary use, herbs can be useful in many other ways. They can be used to either treat or relieve the symptoms of many minor ailments. Many herbal treatments involve making infusions or decoctions or applying compresses and poultices. These are very simple processes, soon mastered with a little practice. In addition, steams, floral water and herb vinegar are among the cosmetic uses herbs can be put to. A bonus of home-made cosmetic and household preparations is that they tend to be less harsh and more environmentally friendly than many of the proprietary products we have become accustomed to using.

typical infusion
Makes 1 cup
1tsp dried herb, or 2tsp fresh

1 Bring 300ml (½pint) filtered water to the boil then pour into a cup. Leave to stand for 30sec.
2 Add the herb, cover and leave to steep for at least 5min, stirring occasionally.
3 Strain the liquid through a piece of muslin and discard the herb. Drink either hot or chilled.

herbal decoction
1tsp dried herb, or 2tsp fresh

1 Crush the herb using a pestle and mortar.
2 Put the crushed herb in a pan and pour in 300ml (½pint) filtered water. Bring to the boil, reduce the heat and simmer gently, covered, for 10min, or until the liquid has reduced to a quarter of its original volume.
3 Strain the liquid through a piece of muslin and discard the herb before using. Drink or use either hot or chilled.

Safety first
Before using herbs medicinally it is important to understand that they must be used sensibly and that they are not automatically safe because they are natural. Even the mildest herbs can cause adverse reactions in some people – so always be careful when using a herb for the first time – even in cooking. If you experience any adverse reaction stop using the herb immediately. Consult a specialist if you are concerned about your condition.

Doctors should be given a complete history of any herbal preparations you are using before any new medication is prescribed or before you undergo any treatment in hospital; herbal preparations can affect your response to conventional drugs. Always consult a qualified herbalist if you are contemplating treating anything other than minor domestic complaints such as coughs, colds and nausea.

Infusions
An infusion involves steeping a fresh or dried herb in boiled water for a period of time – it is basically how we make tea. There is no essential difference between an infusion and a tea, but the latter implies that we are drinking it for pleasure, and the former that it is for medicinal use (whether this be internal or external). The only significant difference here is that an infusion being made for medicinal or cosmetic purposes should be covered with a lid to retain as much of the active ingredients as possible. Timing is also an issue with infusions, which should usually steep for five minutes, whereas when making a herbal tea for pleasure the herb can be left in the water for as long or as little as personal taste dictates.

Herbal infusions can be used to treat a number of different ailments. If you are drinking an infusion for medicinal reasons the dose varies according to the problem. You can drink one cup once a day as a tonic. To treat a minor ailment drink one cup three times a day for two or three days. To treat a chronic problem such as migraine drink one cup three times a day for several weeks. However, do not assume that because herbs are natural substances you can take any amount over any period of time – do follow the appropriate guidelines.

Many fresh herbs can be infused to make delicious and refreshing drinks, or herbal teas, such as rosemary, mint and lemon balm or melissa. Organic dried herbs also make delicious herbal teas, which are entirely different from the proprietary herbal tea mixes on offer at the supermarkets. Lemon verbena, bergamot, rose and chamomile are classics and you can always try blending your own mix. The herbs that are suitable for day-to-day consumption as infusions – or teas – are fairly well known, but do check the Herb Directory before you begin drinking any herb on a regular basis.

Making an infusion
It is best to make herbal infusions daily as required and to use fresh herbs if at all possible, as these are the most potent. However, if you need to use a dried herb remember that one teaspoon of dried herb

is equivalent to two teaspoons of fresh. Exact amounts vary from herb to herb but as a general rule use one teaspoon of herb per cup, that is 300ml (½pint), of water, preferably filtered. Infusions can be kept in the fridge and reheated as required for up to 24 hours.

Most infusions can be taken hot or cold, according to preference, however there are exceptions to this rule and if a temperature is specified for a particular herbal infusion this should always be adhered to. Honey and lemon can be used to further flavour the infusion, or to make treatments more palatable, particularly for young children.

Decoctions

A decoction is an extract of a herb, which is produced by boiling it in water, and is a preparation frequently used for berries, barks and seeds. Whereas herbal infusions are often drunk for pleasure, the function of herbal decoctions is purely medicinal or cosmetic. They can be drunk or used as a gargle, poured into bath water or used in poultices. They are used to treat anything from eczema to cystitis as well as for colouring hair.

To make a decoction you first need to crush the herb to release the active ingredients. Once made, a decoction can be kept in the fridge for up to three days, but ideally it is best to make fresh quantities daily. Use one teaspoon of dried herb per cup or 300ml (½pint) of water, but make up a larger quantity if you need several doses in a single day.

Compresses and poultices

Although the use of poultices and compresses has largely fallen from favour, we do still sometimes use them without realising. When we apply a bag of frozen peas to a bruise or swelling, or a dock leaf to a nettle sting we are, in effect, applying the most basic form of cold compress and poultice. Both types of treatment are effective and useful home remedies.

Compresses

A compress applies infusions or decoctions of plant material and is less messy. To make a hot compress, soak a linen cloth or bandage in a hot infusion or decoction of the appropriate herb, then wrap it around the affected part of the body at as hot a temperature as can be borne. Wrap this with clingfilm and hot towels to maintain the heat.

Cold compresses work similarly, but use chilled ingredients. Puffy and tired eyes benefit from a cold compress of used chamomile or rose-hip tea bags, which have been lightly chilled in the refrigerator. Leave on the eyes for ten minutes.

Poultices

A poultice works in much the same way as a compress, but involves a plant mixture being applied directly to the skin. Mash or crush the plant to release the active ingredients and mix with a little boiling water before applying it to the affected part, again as hot as can be borne. Encase the poultice in a gauze bandage. The vinegar and brown paper referred to in the Jack and Jill nursery rhyme would have been a traditional poultice applied to bring Jack's bruise to the surface of the skin and reduce any swelling. The remedy can still be useful for easing painful bumps and bruising. The poultice should be kept on for four hours at a time and applied twice a day until the swelling and bruising has begun to ease.

Floral water

Before the introduction of commercially produced toiletries, floral waters were once commonly used in the home. They make very gentle face washes and facial steams, and they can be used to perfume hair, clothing or linen. Unfortunately, floral waters do not keep so if you want to use them as a spray to infuse household linens with fragrance, you will need to add alcohol to preserve the scent. Spray on to sheets and pillowcases as you iron them. Floral water can also be used as a fragrant rinse for clothes and linens. To make a rinse, simmer eau de cologne mint, lavender, rose petals or rosemary in a pan of water for 15 minutes. Strain the water and use it as a final rinse when hand-washing clothes, or add to the final rinse cycle of the washing machine. This mixture is quite colourful, however, so it is not suitable for a final rinse when washing whites.

Facial steam

You can make a wonderfully rejuvenating facial steam by simply placing a handful of elderflowers, marigold flowers or rose petals in a heatproof bowl and pouring over boiling water. All you have to do then is lean over the rising steam for approximately ten minutes, covering both your head and the bowl with a towel. The steam increases perspiration, which opens the pores of your skin for a deep cleansing. After the treatment, rinse your face with cold water.

Floral and herb vinegar

Floral vinegars can be used in salads, but they have many other useful applications. They are very refreshing on hot days if dabbed on to sweaty hands and feet, and in France rose vinegar is commonly used for soothing headaches.

Vinegar is beneficial for the condition of both the hair and the scalp and is often recommended as a final hair rinse, so a herb vinegar with its additional herbal properties can be even more beneficial. Sage darkens hair, while chamomile works as a lightener. Rosemary is useful for dry or thinning hair and parsley is said to alleviate dandruff. To make a hair rinse, simply add one tablespoon of herb vinegar to a cup of water and pour over the head. Leave on for five minutes then rinse thoroughly.

Floral vinegar is made in precisely the same way as herb vinegar (*see page 42*), using the same proportions of plant to vinegar, but substituting flower heads or petals for leaves. Other herbs can also be used, including elder, lavender, eau de cologne mint, nasturtium, rose petals, rosemary and thyme.

Floral oil

The flowers of elder, lavender, lemon verbena, rose, rosemary and violet can all be used to make deliciously fragrant oil for a variety of cosmetic uses. A few drops can be added to bath water as a moisturiser, and marigold oil is a good treatment for dry skin on hands and feet. Floral oils are also wonderful scalp and hair conditioners when applied on a weekly basis. Simply warm the oil and massage it into dry hair. Wrap your head in a towel and leave it in place for at least 30 minutes, or overnight. Wash out the oil with shampoo, applying this before wetting your hair with water.

Floral oil is made in the same way as herb oil (*see page 42*), except that almond oil is used as the base oil. Check that the depth of fragrance is to your liking; the oil can be strained and the process repeated to make a stronger perfume. If the oil is for a purely cosmetic purpose, coconut oil can be used, but this will need to be treated differently. Put the coconut oil in a pan, add the dried herb and simmer for five minutes before straining into a container. The mix will solidify but it melts quickly on contact with skin.

herb directory

YARROW

yarrow tea

25g (1oz) fresh yarrow leaves,
or 15g (½oz) dried leaves

1 Put 600ml (1pint) water in a pan and bring to the boil. Remove from the heat and add the herbs. Leave to infuse for 10min.

2 Strain the liquid and discard the herb before drinking or using.

➔ Drink 1 cup two or three times a day for a cold, or use in the bath for up to one week only to soothe and cleanse skin. A mixture of flowers and leaves can be used if preferred.

yarrow facepack

2tbsp fresh yarrow leaves
and flowers
1tsp honey
2tbsp dried milk
1 egg white

1 Pour 300ml (½pint) boiling water over the leaves or flowers. Leave to infuse for 5min.

2 Mix the honey and dried milk together in a bowl, then add 2tbsp yarrow infusion.

3 Whip the egg white until light and frothy then stir into the infusion mixture.

➔ Leave the facepack on your face for 20min then rinse off.

A popular garden plant, yarrow is also a powerful though little-known herb. Its botanical name is believed to have derived from the Greek warrior Achilles, who, according to legend, used the plant to staunch the flow of blood from his soldiers' wounds during the Trojan wars. Indeed, yarrow is thought to possess numerous medical properties, including the ability to help speed up the formation of scar tissue, and it was once widely used to cover cuts and sores. It is undoubtedly a powerful herb – the addition of just a few small leaves will activate and accelerate the decomposition of a wheelbarrowful of raw compost. In ancient times the plant was also used for soothsaying: by the Druids as a means of predicting weather and by the Chinese for foretelling the future in conjunction with their ancient book of divination, the I Ching (The Book of Changes or Yarrow Stalk Oracle).

Yarrow is a hardy perennial indigenous to Europe. It grows in clumps around 60 cm (2ft) tall. The leaves are feathery and have a pleasant smell when crushed. The white or pink flowers grow in flat-topped clusters and bloom all summer. The introduction of yarrow to any herb bed is said to intensify the fragrance, medicinal properties and flavour of nearby herbs. Its root secretions also activate the disease resistance of nearby plants.

To harvest yarrow for drying, gather the leaves and flowers at the commencement of flowering; otherwise use fresh as required.

Do not use yarrow over long periods as it may cause skin irritation, and large doses taken internally can cause headaches and dizziness. Pregnant women should avoid yarrow altogether.

Cultivation

Yarrow is easy to grow. A common wayside plant, it will tolerate most soils and situations. Sow seed in pots in autumn, overwinter in a cool greenhouse and plant out in the garden in spring. As this is an invasive plant sow seed directly into the garden with caution. Yarrow's creeping rootstock makes the plant very easy to propagate by division.

Culinary use

The flavour of the leaves is strong, peppery and bitter. A few chopped leaves added to a cream cheese sandwich is a revelation.

Medicinal use

As it induces perspiration, which lowers temperature and expels toxins, yarrow is reputed to be useful for treating fevers. Yarrow tea, sweetened with honey, acts as a mild diuretic. It is also reputed to help regulate periods, cleanse the system and help to cure a cold. Drink two or three times a day. A decoction used as a mouthwash can soothe inflamed gums. Fresh yarrow leaves applied to wounds are said to be astringent and to have healing properties.

Home and beauty

An infusion of yarrow flowers is said to be useful as a skin-cleansing lotion. Yarrow tea can also be used in the bath, for a limited period of up to one week, to cleanse the skin. A facepack, made with honey and dried milk, is good for greasy skin.

GARLIC

Garlic has been used as a culinary flavouring since ancient times. Originating in central Asia, it became an essential ingredient of many European dishes, notably in the Mediterranean region. The ancient Egyptians, including the pyramid-building slaves, and the Romans used it to sustain their strength. In Greek legend, the hero Odysseus ate wild garlic to foil the enchantress Circe's attempt to transform him into a pig.

For many centuries garlic has also been used medicinally and is known to have both antiseptic and antibiotic properties. It was the main ingredient of Four Thieves' Vinegar, drunk by robbers of dead plague victims as protection against the disease. During the First World War, antiseptic dressings soaked in garlic juice were routinely applied to the wounds of soldiers and are credited with having saved many thousands of lives. The herb is currently the subject of extensive research.

Garlic is a bulbous perennial with a bulb consisting of eight to ten cloves, or segments. The hollow leaves and flower stems can grow to 1.2m (4ft), but are usually shorter. The pink or white flowers bloom from early to mid-summer. Garlic is often used as a companion plant to protect roses from black spot and vulnerable trees from leaf curl.

To harvest garlic, gently remove the bulb from the ground when its leaves die down in mid- to late summer. If possible, allow the bulbs to dry in the sun for a few days, but do not expose them to rain. Plait the bulbs into a rope or put them into a string bag and hang them up. Store garlic in a cool dry room.

garlic decoction

1 head of garlic, divided into cloves and skinned

900ml (1½pints) stock or water

1 Put the garlic in a pan with the stock or water. Bring to the boil, lower the heat and simmer for 10–15min.

2 Allow to cool slightly then strain the liquid and discard the garlic before drinking.

➜ This is delicious when made with stock. Drink 1 cup three times a day to ease hypertension. If you are taking medication for this condition, check with your general practitioner before trying this remedy,

Cultivation

Plant garlic in rich, well-drained soil, in full sun, between the end of autumn and spring. However, tradition holds that it should always be planted on the shortest day of the year and harvested on the longest. Split bulbs into cloves and plant separately, with the pointed end uppermost, 2.5cm (1in) below the surface of the soil and 10cm (4in) apart. Tying the stems into a knot is said to increase the size of the cloves.

Culinary use

Garlic is an indispensable culinary herb with a powerful and distinctive taste and a pervading smell that lingers on chopping boards, fingers and the breath. The cloves are peeled before use then chopped or crushed. Bulbs can be sprinkled around meats when roasting, or slivers can be slotted into incisions in the meat. Garlic can be fried in oil to add flavour to many different dishes, from French to Indian; take care not to cook it in oil or fat that is too hot as this impairs the flavour. Its impact is so strong that merely rubbing a peeled clove around the inside of a salad bowl will impart taste. The freshest garlic tastes the best of all.

Medicinal use

Regular consumption of garlic is said to promote general good health. It is a useful digestive aid, lowers blood pressure and helps regulate the level of cholesterol in the bloodstream. A decoction of garlic is said to help relieve hypertension, but anyone taking medication for hypertension should check with their general practitioner before using one. Garlic is also reputed to ease constipation and to be helpful in the expulsion of catarrh. The aroma of garlic tends to linger on the breath; if this is a problem try chewing some parsley or chervil.

AÏOLI

Makes about 300ml (½pint)

4 garlic cloves, peeled

2 egg yolks

300ml (½pint) olive oil

30ml (2tbsp) lemon juice

1 Crush the garlic with ¼ level tsp salt
using a pestle and mortar. Add the egg
yolks and beat well.

2 Add the oil, one drop at a time, beating
well after each addition until the mixture
is thick and smooth. Add the lemon juice
to taste.

CHIVES

A member of the onion family, chives are an incredibly useful herb, especially in the kitchen. The tubular leaves have a pungent and distinctive onion taste and smell, which make a wonderful addition to a range of dishes. Indigenous to Europe, Asia and north-east America, the plant was introduced to Britain by the Romans. Chives are also known to have been used in China as long ago as 3000BC.

This hardy perennial grows naturally in the wild in dry, rocky situations. It is a low-growing herb, with an average height of 15cm (6in), which looks very effective planted along the edge of a path. If allowed to flower, the tufted pink flower heads are appealing and herald the start of summer. Chives are also useful in the vegetable plot as companion plants to deter aphids.

Harvest the leaves by cutting them as required. Grow several clumps and use one at a time, leaving at least 5cm (2in) for regrowth. The leaves freeze well in ice cubes. To keep a year-round supply of fresh herb, take one or two small clumps from the garden and place in a 10cm (4in) pot to keep on the kitchen windowsill.

Cultivation

Chives are satisfyingly easy to grow. They enjoy a good garden soil in a sunny or partially shaded position. They can be sown from seed in spring, but germination is slow and once a bed is established it is easier to increase stock by division. Every three years lift and divide older plants and replant 23cm (9in) apart. Given the right growing conditions chives will self-seed freely and can become a bit of a nuisance. They are useful plants to grow in containers positioned close to the kitchen door.

Culinary use

Chives bring a subtle onion flavour to mild dishes and are delicious chopped into omelettes or snipped over new potatoes and salads. They also make a delicious herb butter, which is wonderful on warm French bread; prepare it at least one hour before use to allow the flavour to fully infuse the butter. As chives do not respond well to heat, they are best added to cooked food when the process is completed. Chives taste best before the plant begins to flower in early summer.

Medicinal use

Reputed to both stimulate the appetite and aid digestion, chives are also claimed to act as a mild laxative and a sedative. They contain some vitamin C and some iron. Like their close relative, garlic, chives are believed to be mildly antibiotic as well as antifungal.

PARMESAN AND CHIVE ROLLS

Makes 8

450g (1lb) strong plain white flour, sifted,
plus extra for dusting
7g (¼oz) sachet fast-action dried yeast
Pinch of sugar
4tbsp freshly chopped chives
60g (2½oz) freshly grated Parmesan
cheese
300ml (½pint) milk
25g (1oz) butter, plus extra for greasing

1 Put the flour and 1 level tsp salt in a bowl and stir in the yeast, sugar, chives, and all but 15g (½oz) of the cheese.
2 Heat the milk and butter in a small pan until the butter has melted; allow to cool slightly until tepid. Gradually add to the dry ingredients and work together to form a soft dough.
3 Knead for 8–10min until smooth, then put in a greased bowl. Cover and leave to rise in a warm place for 1hr.
4 Punch the dough to knock out the air and divide into 8 pieces. Shape into balls, flatten slightly and put on a large oiled baking sheet. Cover loosely and leave to rise for 30min.
5 Sprinkle the remaining Parmesan over the rolls and bake at 220ºC (200ºC in a fan oven), mark 7 for 15–20min until risen and golden. Cool on a wire rack.

LEMON VERBENA

lemon verbena tea

25g (1oz) fresh lemon verbena
leaves or flowers, or 15g (½oz)
dried leaves or flowers

1 Put 600ml (1pint) water in a pan and
bring to the boil. Remove from the heat
and add the lemon verbena leaves or
flowers. Leave to infuse for 5min.
2 Strain the liquid and discard the
lemon verbena before drinking.
➔ Drink 1 cup three times a day as
a calmative.

A native of Chile and Peru, lemon verbena is a beautiful aromatic plant, its leaves having
a sharp smell of lemon. The Spanish introduced it to Europe in the eighteenth century for
the manufacture of perfume. The essence extracted from the leaves is still commonly
used in perfumes and liqueur.

Lemon verbena is a tender deciduous shrub that grows 1.5m (5ft) high. Its
lance-shaped green leaves are arranged in groups of three. New growth can appear
quite late in the season, so never give up on a plant until late summer. The small panicles
of lavender-coloured flowers open in mid- and late summer.

To harvest lemon verbena, pick both leaves and flowers just before the flowers
open. This is an easy herb to dry and the scent is retained for some time. Once dried,
store in an airtight container.

Take care not to confuse this herb with the similarly named herbaceous plant
vervain, or verbena, which has quite different properties.

Cultivation

Lemon verbena is happiest in a
poor soil and prefers a warm, damp climate. It requires a very sheltered, sunny
position and protection throughout winter.
Covering the roots with wood ash, straw
or leaf-mould will suffice where winters
are not too harsh. However, it will not survive severe winters and will need to be
dug up every autumn and placed in a
pot to overwinter in a cool greenhouse.
Lemon verbena is best propagated by
stem cuttings, which can be taken during
spring, summer and early autumn. If
growing from seed, sow in spring and
keep warm. Keep the new plants under
cover until they are two years old before
planting out in the garden. Space the
plants 1m (3ft) apart. If you prefer, lemon
verbena can be grown entirely in containers, as long as these are a minimum size
of 20cm (8in). Place the containers in a
sunny spot and feed the plants throughout the growing season.

Culinary use

The leaves are very flavoursome,
with a sweet, lemony-perfumed tang –
use them with a light hand. Try adding
freshly chopped leaves to home-made
vanilla ice cream, or use crushed leaves
to flavour oil or vinegar.

Medicinal use

You can use a lemon verbena leaf
infusion, or tea, as a calmative. The herb
is also believed to be helpful in treating
nausea, indigestion and flatulence.

Home and beauty

As the aromatic leaves of lemon
verbena retain their strong fragrance for
some years, they are useful for inclusion
in potpourri and herb pillow mixes. They
will also make a bath fragrant and uplifting: simply put the leaves in a muslin bag
and position it under the warm water tap
when you run the water. To make scented
massage oil, add leaves to some almond
oil and leave to infuse. This herb will
soothe tired, puffy eyes: soak cotton wool
pads in a cooled infusion, or tea, and
place on the eyelids for ten minutes.

LEMON SORBET

Serves 3–4

3 lemons, preferably organic
125g (4oz) golden caster sugar
1 medium egg white
Lemon verbena, for decorating

1 Finely pare the zest from the lemons using a citrus zester, then squeeze the lemon for its juice. Put the zest in a pan with the caster sugar and 350ml (12fl oz) water and heat gently to dissolve. Increase the heat and boil for 10min.
2 Leave the sugar syrup to cool, then stir in the lemon juice. Cover the pan and chill for 30min.
3 Strain the syrup through a fine sieve into a bowl. In another bowl, beat the egg white until just frothy, then whisk into the lemon mixture.
4 For optimum results, freeze in an ice-cream maker. Alternatively, pour into a shallow freezerproof container and freeze until the sorbet is almost frozen; mash well with a fork and refreeze until solid.
5 Transfer to the fridge for 30min before serving to soften slightly. Decorate with lemon verbena before serving.

MARSH MALLOW

marsh mallow milk

25g (1oz) freshly grated marsh
    mallow root
600ml (1pint) milk
1–2tbsp honey, to taste

1 Put all the ingredients in a pan and
bring gently to the boil. Lower the heat
and simmer gently for 30min.
→ Take 1 tablespoon three times a
day to relieve hoarse coughs and
gastric ulcers.

Marsh mallow is a pretty herb, famous for its softening and healing properties. It is the plant from which the famous spongy sweet takes its name. Indigenous to Britain, central and southern Europe and North Africa, it was used in ancient times as a medicinal plant. The botanical name *Althaea* comes from the Greek word *altho*, which means 'to cure'. The early Egyptians, Greeks and Romans also considered marsh mallow a culinary delicacy and often included it in barley soup and the stuffing for suckling pigs. The root and leaves contain the valuable thickening and softening mucilage, or sticky gum, and it is this substance that provides the herb with a range of medicinal applications.

A hardy perennial plant, marsh mallow carries velvety, grey-green heart-shaped leaves on tall stems that will easily reach 1m (3ft). The pink or white flowers are borne from late summer to early autumn.

To harvest, pick fresh leaves for immediate use, or cut them for drying. The roots can be harvested after two years and can be used fresh or dried.

lotion for dry hands

25g (1oz) freshly grated marsh
    mallow root
2tbsp ground almonds
1dssp milk
1tsp cider vinegar

1 Place the grated marsh mallow root
in a bowl.
2 Pour over 150ml (¼pint) cold water
and leave to soak for 24 hours.
3 Strain the liquid and put 1tbsp liquid
into a container. Add the ground
almonds, milk and cider vinegar and
beat together until well mixed.
→ This makes a runny, slightly gritty
solution. Store in an airtight container in
the fridge and use within five days.

Cultivation
Marsh mallow thrives in seaside situations, preferring full sun and a moist or wet soil. Seeds can be sown in autumn and left to overwinter in a cold frame; they will germinate in the spring. When the seedlings are big enough to handle, plant them out 45cm (18in) apart. Lift and divide established plants in either autumn or spring.

Culinary use
The sweet roots, which produce the flavouring that was originally used for marshmallow sweets, are delicious as a vegetable. Boil a root for a few minutes, peel and fry gently in a little butter.

Medicinal use
Marsh mallow soothes and relieves inflammation and ulceration of the stomach and small intestine. It also helps relieves the pain of sore throats and cystitis. An infusion of the root is reputed to quieten coughs, stop diarrhoea and overcome insomnia. An infusion of the flowers can be used as a soothing gargle.

Home and beauty
The mucilage in the marsh mallow root gives the plant its effective softening and healing properties. Decoctions of root and leaves applied externally or used for facial steams can help relieve mild sunburn. Marsh mallow is a useful ingredient for hand cream for both soothing and moisturising the skin.

DILL

dill water

15g (¹/₂oz) dried dill seeds

1 Bruise the dill seeds using a pestle and mortar, then put them in a heatproof bowl.

2 Put 300ml (½pint) water in a pan and bring to the boil. Remove from the heat and add to the bruised seeds. Leave to infuse for 10min.

3 Strain the liquid and discard the seeds. Allow to cool.

➜ Give babies 1 teaspoon as required.

Dill has an established reputation as a culinary and medicinal herb. Its soothing powers are the basis of gripe water, or dill water, which is used to treat babies suffering from colic. The name is derived from the Norse *dilla* or the Anglo-Saxon *dylle*, which both mean 'to lull' or 'to soothe', and the plant has been employed medicinally since ancient times – early Egyptian physicians were using it over 5000 years ago. Dill is mentioned in the Bible, and during the Middle Ages it was used right across northern Europe. It is still a popular culinary herb, most notably in Scandinavia.

Resembling fennel in appearance, dill is a very pretty hardy annual. It grows to around 60cm (2ft) or more in height, carrying bright green, feathery foliage and bearing umbels, or flat heads, of tiny yellow flowers from early to mid-summer.

You can pick the leaves once the plant is mature, about two months after sowing. As the greenery does not dry easily, it is better to preserve the seed for later use. Simply hang the flower heads upside down in a warm, dry room, with a paper bag tied over them to catch the seeds when they fall. After a week detach any remaining seeds and store in an airtight container.

Cultivation

Dill enjoys well-drained soil in full sun. Sow seeds in drills, from mid-spring to early summer, where it is to flower, as the herb does not like being transplanted. Thin the seedlings to 23cm (9in) apart. Once dill flowers it is of no use as a fresh herb as all its strength goes into seed production, so to keep a continual supply of greenery sow seeds at fortnightly intervals. Dill self-seeds freely given the right growing conditions. It is best not to grow dill close to fennel as the plants cross-pollinate and hybrid seeds will result. Dill can be grown in a container; ideally it should be cut continually for use, but will need to be staked if grown to flower.

Culinary use

Dill is the essential ingredient in *gravadlax*, the famous Scandinavian salmon dish. The herb has a sharp, sweet taste that offsets any blandness in the fish without overwhelming it. However, the greenery loses something of its distinctive flavour on cooking, so always add to a hot dish at the last possible moment. Use freshly chopped leaves as a garnish and in sauces for fish dishes. They are also delicious chopped into soured cream or mixed into salads. Try boiling it with new potatoes instead of mint. Dill is also widely used to flavour pickling vinegar. The flat brown seeds, which split into two, have a distinctive, bitter taste that suits pickles. Dill is rich in mineral salts so the seeds, used whole or ground, can offer a useful alternative to salt for anyone following a salt-free diet.

Medicinal use

Like fennel, aniseed and caraway, dill aids digestion by stimulating the flow of digestive juices. However, as it is a very mild herb it can be safely used to calm the painful wind, or colic, that torments some tiny infants. Nursing mothers can help soothe a baby's tummy by dosing themselves with one tablespoon, thus treating the baby indirectly via the milk.

The seeds are said to have a sedative effect and can help stave off hunger.

Home and beauty

As well as acting as a digestive, dill seeds are said to sweeten the breath if chewed. Try serving up a platter of seeds after a rich or spicy meal.

GRAVADLAX WITH POTATO AND DILL SALAD

Serves 6

40g (1½oz) coarse sea salt
50g (2oz) caster sugar
25g (1oz) freshly chopped dill
2 level tsp English mustard powder
50ml (2fl oz) vodka
550g (1¼lb) skinned salmon tail end fillet

For the Potato and Dill Salad

4 level tbsp mayonnaise
2tbsp lemon juice
1 level tsp caster sugar
2 level tbsp freshly chopped dill
1tbsp olive oil
450g (1lb) scrubbed new potatoes

To garnish

Sliced cucumber
Chopped spring onions
Grated lemon rind

1 To make the marinade, mix the salt, sugar, dill, mustard powder and vodka in a bowl. Season with freshly ground black pepper. Put the salmon in a shallow dish and spoon over the marinade. Cover with clingfilm, place a board or plate then two heavy weights or cans on top and chill for at least 48hr. Turn and baste the salmon with the marinade from time to time.

2 To make the Potato and Dill Salad, combine the mayonnaise, lemon juice, sugar, dill, olive oil and freshly ground black pepper together in a bowl; whisk until smooth. Cook the potatoes in boiling, salted water, then drain. Cool and slice then toss in the mayonnaise. The salad will keep in the fridge for 24hr.

3 Remove the salmon from the dish and cut into thin slices. Garnish with sliced cucumber, chopped spring onions and grated lemon rind, and serve with the Potato and Dill Salad.

ANGELICA

Angelica is one of the giants of the herb garden often reaching an imposing 2.4m (8ft) in a single season. It was once considered a protection against witchcraft and its name is derived from the reputed date of flowering – the feast day of Michael the Archangel on 8 May. Indigenous to Europe, North America and Asia, angelica was once in frequent and wide use as a medicine that could cure all manner of illnesses. Today the herb has been relegated to the role of mere cake decoration although it can offer plenty more. The young stems can be used as a sweetening agent and are especially valuable when cooking acid fruits, such as gooseberries, rhubarb and plums, in desserts or jams. The seeds are much used commercially as a flavouring in liqueurs like Chartreuse. The whole plant is deliciously fragrant and the essential oil is used in the perfume industry and for potpourri. In addition, angelica is said to be helpful for treating respiratory conditions and for stimulating appetite.

A short-lived perennial usually grown as a biennial, angelica has fat, ridged hollow stems that bear large, bright green serrated leaves. The yellowish-green flowers appear in clusters from mid- to late summer in the plant's second year. The seed is pale yellow when ripe.

Harvest the leaves for use fresh as required. For drying, pick the leaves before flowering begins. Gather the flowers in early summer for drying, and the seeds as they ripen. For making crystallised angelica, pick stems while the plant is very young.

Cultivation

Angelica needs a lot of space and enjoys partial shade and a good, rich moist soil. It is easy to grow from seed, but as the seed quickly loses viability it is best sown fresh in the autumn. Sow seeds where they are to flower, as the seedlings do not readily transplant, and thin seedlings to allow approximately 1m (3ft) between plants. The young plants will die back completely over winter before re-emerging the following spring.

Culinary use

Angelica can be used to flavour mayonnaise; try mixing freshly chopped dill and mint leaves into the mayonnaise and use in sandwiches. However, the herb is usually associated with the crystallised stems that are used in cake decoration.

Medicinal use

Angelica is thought to relieve flatulence, indigestion and rheumatism, and can act as a tonic for anyone suffering from a cold. A tea made from fresh leaves will relieve tension headaches and colds. An infusion made from root or dried seeds is useful for severe colds and bronchial problems. You need only one cupful a day, as the mixture can initially stimulate and then depress the nervous system; anyone suffering from diabetes should not try this. Placing crushed leaves in the car is said to prevent travel sickness.

Home and beauty

Place fresh leaves in a muslin bag and hang under running water to make a relaxing bath. Crushed fresh leaves act as an air freshener.

CRYSTALLISED ANGELICA STEMS

Very young angelica stems, cut diagonally
    into short lengths
Golden granulated sugar

1 Bring a pan of water to the boil, add the
angelica stems and simmer until soft, but
not pulpy.
2 Remove the stems from the water and
when cool enough to handle, remove the
outer skin.
3 Return the stems to the pan and
simmer until bright green in colour.
4 Remove and dry the stems. Weigh the
stems, put in a shallow dish and sprinkle
with an equivalent weight of sugar. Toss
to cover completely and leave for 2 days.
5 Put the angelica and sugar in a pan and
simmer for 10min.
6 Remove the stems from the pan and
dry on racks. Store in an airtight container
on greaseproof paper.

Note: If the angelica is not completely dry
it will deteriorate rapidly.

CHERVIL

Chervil is a magnificent culinary herb with a delicate perfumed flavour that deserves to be more widely grown and used than it is in Britain. It is favoured in French cuisine, however, and along with parsley, tarragon and chives is an essential component of the classic *fines herbes* mix (*see page 138*). A native of the Middle East and south-eastern Europe, chervil is believed to have been introduced to Britain by the Romans. It is reputed to have blood-cleansing and restorative properties and is one of the Lenten herbs, traditionally used on Maundy Thursday.

Resembling immature cow parsley, chervil is a very pretty annual, which can grow 60cm (2ft) high. Its lacy fern-like leaves are bright green. The flowers grow in small white clusters from the end of spring through summer.

Harvest leaves before the plant flowers, after which the plant has no further culinary use. The leaves are at their best when used fresh, and you can pick them as soon as the plant is mature. Although the leaves lose their flavour when dried, they can be frozen successfully.

Cultivation

Chervil grows best in moist soil in semi-shade; if grown in sunshine it flowers all too quickly. It does not like being transplanted so scatter the seed in drills where it is to grow or sow in pots from late spring to early summer. It can also be sown in between the taller vegetable plants, where it will enjoy the shaded conditions. The seed germinates rapidly in warm soil and plants are ready for use in six to eight weeks. To ensure a constant supply of fresh leaves sow at regular intervals throughout the summer. Chervil makes a good container plant in the summer; however, it tends to become leggy when grown indoors.

Culinary use

Chervil can be used in the kitchen only before flowering. It has a delicate parsley flavour combined with a dash of aniseed that complements salads, soups, sauces, chicken, and egg and fish dishes. It is best added to hot dishes immediately before serving as cooking impairs its flavour. Sprinkle it chopped over vegetables or use as a garnish. Chervil also makes good herb vinegar.

Medicinal use

This herb is rich in vitamin C, iron, carotene and magnesium. Infuse leaves to make a tea that will improve digestion and ease catarrh, liver complaints and circulatory problems; it will also act as a mild diuretic. An infusion used as a compress or eyewash will soothe tired, irritated eyes. Fresh leaves can be used to make a poultice that will ease aching joints.

Home and beauty

An infusion made from the leaves is reputed to be a pleasant cleanser for mature skins.

CHERVIL SOUP

Serves 4

75g (3oz) butter
2 leeks, washed and chopped
1 onion, chopped
2 large potatoes, peeled and chopped
1.1 litres (2pints) boiling stock or water
2 level tsp dried chervil or 2tbsp freshly
    chopped chervil

1 Melt 50g (2oz) of the butter in a pan
and gently fry the leeks and onion until
soft and transparent. Add the potatoes
and the stock or water and season with
salt and freshly ground black pepper to
taste. Add the dried chervil, if using. Bring
the soup to the boil and simmer slowly for
at least 30min.

2 Whiz the vegetables and stock in a
blender until smooth. Return to the pan,
season and heat gently. Add the fresh
chervil, if using, and serve immediately.

HORSERADISH

horseradish syrup

40g (1½oz) freshly chopped
    horseradish root
450g (1lb) golden granulated sugar
    or honey

1 Put the chopped horseradish root in
a pan with 900ml (1½pints) water and
bring gently to the boil. Reduce the
heat, cover and simmer gently for
20min. Remove from the heat and
allow to cool.
2 Strain the liquid into another pan
and discard the root. Return the liquid
to the heat and simmer, uncovered,
until reduced to 200ml (7fl oz).
3 Add the sugar or honey, allow to
dissolve slowly then simmer gently
for 2–3min, stirring continuously, until
syrupy.
→ For a persistent cough, adults may
take 2 teaspoons three times a day.
The dose for children is 1 teaspoon
three times a day.

The root of horseradish has an incredibly strong, pungent flavour. The plant is no beauty, but the flavour contained in its roots makes it very worthwhile to cultivate. Native to south-eastern Europe and western Asia, it was originally used as a medicinal herb. The plant has antibiotic properties and was formerly associated with the treatment of urinary tract infections and respiratory complaints. Its principal appeal today is as a culinary herb where its distinctive hot, sharp, biting flavour is invaluable in sauces or as an accompaniment to many dishes. In Britain its most traditional form is as a sauce accompaniment to roast beef. The Danes and the Germans have made more of it, using it as an alternative to mustard and serving it grated raw with roast beef, as a sauce accompaniment for mackerel and herring, or mixed with stewed apples to make a complementary sauce for duck or goose.

Horseradish is a perennial herb frequently found growing wild. It is very easy to grow, indeed given the right conditions it will take over. It grows 60cm (2ft) tall and has wavy-edged leaves that look a little like an elongated dock leaf. The small white flowers bloom from mid- to late summer. The long white taproot contains vitamin C, calcium, magnesium and sodium. Horseradish can be grown near potatoes as a companion plant to improve the disease resistance of the tubers.

To harvest, dig up the roots at any time for fresh use. To store the roots, dig them up in autumn, cover with sand and keep in a cool, dark place. Alternatively, wash the roots carefully and store them in white wine vinegar. Leaves are best picked when they are young, either to use fresh or for drying.

Cultivation

Horseradish likes an open, sunny situation in rich, moist soil. The easiest method of propagation is by division in spring; the smallest pieces of root will grow. If you want to start your own plants, find someone who already has a clump ask them to lift and divide. You can also use root division to increase stock. In spring cut a root into 15cm (6in) pieces and plant them directly in the ground 30cm (12in) apart. Take great care if sowing seed as the resulting crop could run out of control.

Culinary use

The strongest flavour comes from roots pulled in autumn; spring roots are much milder. Prepare the horseradish root by peeling then grating it. Take great care when grating the root – you may want to wear protective glasses or goggles because the sap will sting if it gets in your eyes. To make a horseradish sauce you can mix it with whipped cream, soured cream or vinegar. It can also be mixed into coleslaw. Horseradish root does not respond well to cooking. The young leaves are very tasty added to a salad.

Medicinal use

Horseradish stimulates the circulatory system and is an effective diuretic and nasal decongestant. It can help in the treatment of gout and rheumatism. Eating the root is beneficial and horseradish syrup is a good treatment for persistent coughs. A poultice made from the grated root is said to soothe chilblains, sciatica, rheumatism and stiff muscles. Overuse of horseradish can cause the skin to blister, though, so the poultice should be used for short periods only. Pregnant women and anyone suffering from kidney problems should treat this herb with caution.

Home and beauty

Infusing slices of the root in milk is said to produce a lotion which, if used occasionally, will improve skin clarity and brighten tired grey skin. It is very astringent, however, so is not suitable for anyone with sensitive skin. Chopped horseradish leaves added to dog food are reputed to help expel parasitic worms.

HOT BEETROOT WITH HORSERADISH

Serves 4–6

450g (1lb) cooked beetroot
1 level tbsp golden caster sugar
4tbsp red wine vinegar
2tbsp freshly grated horseradish
1tbsp cornflour

1 Rub the skin off the beetroot carefully using your fingers. Slice the beetroot neatly into rounds.

2 Put the beetroot in a large heavy-based pan, then sprinkle with the sugar. Pour in the red wine vinegar and add the horse-radish. Season with salt and freshly ground black pepper.

3 Bring to the boil, without stirring, then lower the heat, cover and simmer gently for 10min.

4 Transfer the beetroot slices carefully to a warmed serving dish using a slotted spoon. Mix the cornflour to a paste with a little cold water, then stir into the cooking liquid in the pan. Boil for 1–2min, stirring vigorously until the liquid thickens. To serve, taste and adjust the seasoning, then pour the sauce over the beetroot. Serve immediately.

TARRAGON

tarragon digestif

900ml (1½pints) 40% or 50%
alcohol, such as vodka
25g (1oz) fresh tarragon leaves
1 vanilla pod
350g (12oz) golden granulated
sugar

1 Pour the alcohol into a jar and add
the remaining ingredients. Seal and
leave to infuse for one month, shaking
occasionally during that time.
2 Strain the liquid and discard the
tarragon and vanilla before drinking.

No self-respecting herb garden should be without tarragon. It is an important culinary herb and an essential ingredient in classic French cuisine. The herb is indigenous to Russia, Siberia, Mongolia, northern China and western and central North America. Both its botanical name, *dracunculus*, and its common name, which comes from the French *estragon*, mean 'little dragon'. It is believed that the name derives from a time when tarragon was regarded as an effective treatment for the bites of venomous creatures and mad dogs. Other explanations are that the name refers to the hot taste of the herb or the coiled shape of its roots. Like other wormwoods, such as the silvery garden favourite *Artemisia absinthium* (the bitter, aromatic basis of the addictive liqueur *absinthe*), this herb has a stimulating effect on the digestive system, yet calms indigestion and hiccups. Tarragon leaves are rich in vitamins A and C, as well as iodine and mineral salts.

Tarragon is a half-hardy perennial that grows 1m (3ft) high. It has shiny, narrow aromatic leaves and tiny yellow flowers, which bloom from mid- to late summer. The plant spreads by a network of underground runners, which can be as long as 1m (3ft).

Pick the leaves to use fresh as required throughout the summer. Do not cut more than two-thirds of a branch at any one time unless it is the end of the growing season. To harvest for freezing, it is best to gather leaves in mid-summer. Tarragon is not a good candidate for drying as its leaves lose much of their flavour during the process.

Cultivation

Tarragon enjoys a sunny situation in good, well-drained soil. It is unlikely to set seed in temperate climates so is best propagated by taking cuttings or root division. As the herb is not fully hardy, it needs some protection in severe winters; cut down plants and protect from frosts with a deep mulch of straw, leaves or agricultural fleece. Tarragon is a good container plant and can be overwintered in a cool, protected spot.

Culinary use

Tarragon is a useful herb with a warm faintly aniseed flavour. The chopped leaves or young leafy stalks are delicious added to anything from roast meat to poultry and fish. They will also give a little emphasis to mildly flavoured vegetables, such as artichokes and marrows. Tarragon vinegar, perfect for making a French dressing, is very easy to make: simply steep the tarragon in boiled white wine vinegar. Tarragon is also an essential ingredient in *béarnaise* and *hollandaise* sauces and *sauce tartare*. When purchasing the herb for culinary use take care to buy French tarragon and not Russian tarragon (*Artemisia dracunculus dracunculoides*), which has less flavour and a coarser texture.

Medicinal use

Tarragon is said to be helpful for treating all sorts of digestive disturbances from nausea to flatulence as well as rheumatism, gout and arthritis. Drink a small glass of the *digestif* after a meal.

Home and beauty

Chewing tarragon leaves is said to sweeten the breath. If chewed before taking unpleasant-tasting medicine, they are reputed to dull the taste.

BÉARNAISE SAUCE

Serves 4

For the herb vinegar

4tbsp white wine vinegar

6 peppercorns

1 bay leaf

½ level tsp dried tarragon or 1½ level tsp
    freshly chopped tarragon

½ level tsp dried chervil or 1½ level tsp
    freshly chopped chervil

1 shallot, chopped

For the béarnaise sauce

2 egg yolks

75g (3oz) unsalted butter, softened

½ level tsp dried tarragon or 1½ level tsp
    freshly chopped tarragon

½ level tsp dried chervil or 1½ level tsp
    freshly chopped chervil

4tbsp double cream, lightly whipped

1 Put all the ingredients for the herb vinegar in a pan, bring to the boil and bubble
gently to reduce to 1tbsp. Strain the vinegar into the top of a double saucepan.

2 Blend the egg yolks with a knob of the
softened butter, then add to the vinegar.

3 Heat the water in the bottom of the
double saucepan to simmering. Stir the
egg yolk mixture with a wooden spoon
until it begins to thicken. Add the butter, a
knob at a time, gradually increasing the
heat. When all the butter is added, stir in
the herbs and cream, and season with
salt and freshly ground black pepper to
taste. Cover and keep warm.

ORACH

Also known as mountain spinach, orach is an underrated herb in Britain but is widely used in Europe, where it is cooked like spinach, to which family it belongs. The red variety is the most popular for culinary use and is certainly worth trying if you enjoy sampling exotic leafy vegetables. Its origins are unknown, but it is found growing right across Europe. The herb was widely grown in England during the Middle Ages, but is now rarely cultivated although it can still be found growing wild.

Orach is a giant of an annual, reaching an impressive 2m (6ft) in height in a single season. It is strikingly handsome and worth growing for its looks alone. The arrow- or heart-shaped leaves are green or red and tiny green or red flowers appear throughout summer and well into autumn. It can make a striking container plant.

Pick leaves when young to use fresh as required. Orach does not dry or freeze very successfully.

Cultivation

Orach is easy to grow but needs a good rich garden soil. Red orach prefers partial shade as its leaves tend to scorch in sun. Sow seed in drills 60cm (2ft) apart when all danger of frost has passed. The plant runs to seed easily so pick off the flower heads as they form. However, successive sowings offer the best route to a constant supply throughout the summer. Water the plants well for good growth.

Culinary use

Older orach leaves become bitter and tough so ideally use only the young leaves of this herb. The appeal for me is more visual than taste – a few of these leaves transform the look of a dreary salad. Combined with potatoes, garlic and a vegetable or chicken stock, orach leaves also make a good soup.

Medicinal use

Orach acts as a calmative for indigestion and hysteria and is effective when taken as an infusion, although it does taste rather unpleasant. Like spinach, it contains vitamin C and iron.

BORAGE

Borage is a pretty garden herb. It is indigenous to the Mediterranean region, but is now naturalised in Europe and North America, to which it was taken by early settlers. In the ancient world it was believed to have a strong impact on the body by instilling courage, dispelling despair and inducing a sense of wellbeing. The Greeks and Romans used it extensively and it may have been mixed with wine to make a drink known as *nepenthe*, which Homer said brought about a state of absolute forgetfulness. Modern research has shown that borage works on the adrenal gland, which affects the body's response in a crisis, which may explain its heroic reputation. Its high content of calcium, potassium and mineral salts make it a good blood purifier and general tonic.

The blue flowers are much admired. They were floated as decoration in the stirrup cups of crusaders as they set out for the Holy Land, and their intense colour is said to have inspired old masters when painting the robes of the Madonna.

Borage is an easily cultivated annual that grows 50cm (20in) high. The leaves and stems are rough and covered with stiff, prickly white hairs. The clusters of starry, bright blue flowers appear from early summer through to autumn. Bees favour the flowers, which makes borage a useful companion plant for vegetables that rely on insects for pollination, notably runner beans and strawberries. Blackfly are also attracted to it, so nearby plants often remain pest free.

Pick flowers for use fresh as required, but for freezing or crystallising harvest them when they have just opened. Pick young leaves fresh for immediate use only.

Cultivation

Borage prefers a sunny position in a light, well-drained soil. Sow seeds directly into the flowering position, as this herb does not like being transplanted. Thin seedlings to leave 30cm (12 in) between plants. Plants will readily self-seed in the right conditions.

Culinary use

The young leaves have a pleasant taste reminiscent of cucumber and are delicious chopped and tossed in a salad. The stiff hairs on the leaves seem to dissolve rapidly in the mouth. The flowers make a pretty garnish. They can be floated decoratively on drinks or frozen in ice cubes to be served in cool summer beverages. The crystallised flowers make delightful decorations for desserts or cakes. As borage is rich in mineral salts, it can be a useful herb for anyone following a salt-free diet. However, as it can be toxic if taken to excess, take medical advice before using it for this purpose.

Medicinal use

Borage is an anti-inflammatory and a mild diuretic. The whole plant contains mucilage, which gives it many soothing properties. Syrup, for instance, is helpful in the treatment of bladder and kidney infections. Hot borage tea is useful for reducing temperatures and relieving catarrh. Drunk hot or cold, the tea is also said to reduce stress. A poultice made from the leaves soothes bruises and inflammation.

Home and beauty

Borage can be used to make a facial steam to soothe dry sensitive skin. Just sprinkle two tablespoons of freshly chopped borage leaves into a large heat-proof bowl and pour over a couple of litres of freshly boiled water. Lean over the bowl, your head covered with a towel and your eyes closed, for ten minutes.

BORAGE AND PARMESAN FRITTERS

Serves 4; makes 16–20

50g (2oz) fresh white breadcrumbs
65g (2½oz) fresh borage leaves
15g (½oz) butter
4 medium eggs
2 level tbsp finely grated Parmesan
    cheese
1 small garlic clove, finely chopped
Sunflower or olive oil, for frying

1 Preheat the oven to 110°C (90°C in a fan oven), mark ¼. Spread the bread-crumbs over a large baking sheet and bake for 15–20min until dry but not coloured. Cool.
2 Meanwhile, roll up the borage leaves and chop into wide strips. Melt the butter in a large pan, add the borage leaves and cook over a medium-high heat until wilted. Tip on to a board and chop finely.
3 Put the eggs in a bowl and beat until slightly frothy. Stir in the breadcrumbs, Parmesan cheese, chopped borage leaves, garlic and season with salt and freshly ground black pepper.
4 Pour oil into a large deep frying pan to a depth of 2.5cm (1in) and heat over a medium-high heat to 180°C or until a cube of bread browns in 20sec. Drop heaped teaspoonfuls of batter into the oil and cook for 3min, turning now and then, until the fritters are crisp and golden. Remove with a slotted spoon and drain briefly on kitchen paper. Sprinkle with sea salt and serve immediately.

MUSTARD

Mustard has been used as an essential flavouring in cooking and as a medicinal herb for many thousands of years. Indigenous to the Middle East, it is now naturalised in Britain and America. The Romans soaked pounded mustard seed in wine to produce a drink they called *mustus* and in consequence the herb acquired its common name of mustard – a combination of *mustus* and *ardens*, which means 'fiery'. Mustard was also believed to have aphrodisiac powers and so was used in many love potions.

Black mustard (*Brassica nigra*), named after the black colour of the seed, has the strongest-flavoured seed of the three mustard species. Brown mustard (*B. juncea*) is easier to harvest mechanically; the flavour of its seed is not released until ground and mixed with a liquid. White mustard (*B. alba*) is used to form the mustard part of the fresh mustard and cress salad crop.

Mustard is a hardy annual and resembles its close relative, rape (*B. napus*), which can be seen flowering in fields in late spring. Given the right conditions it can reach a towering 2.4m (8 ft) in height. The branching stems carry oval leaves, and clusters of small yellow flowers appear from early to mid-summer.

To harvest seed for drying, pick the seed pods before they open in late summer. Pick young leaves for salads just eight to ten days after sowing and gather flowers as they open.

Cultivation

Mustard enjoys a sunny situation in well-drained soil, though it can benefit from a little shade to discourage the plants from bolting. Sow in spring for a seed crop, or sow seeds every three weeks for use fresh in salads.

Culinary use

Mustard leaves are deliciously pungent in salads. The flowers are also edible and can be used in sandwiches or tossed into salads. To make mustard, grind dried seed and add water to make a thick paste. Leave for ten minutes before use to allow the flavour to develop fully. The mixture does not keep, so make mustard fresh as required.

Medicinal use

Powdered mustard makes an effective poultice for the relief of inflammation and pain caused by rheumatism and arthritis. A mustard foot bath will warm and refresh tired feet. Add two teaspoons of mustard powder to approximately 2litres (4pints) of hot water and mix in a basin large enough to place both feet together. Sit down with both feet in the bath and relax for 15 minutes. Mustard can also be used as an emetic.

Home and beauty

Mustard is said to have a useful deodorising action. To remove strong odours, such as garlic or methylated spirits, from your hands rub pounded seeds into them and rinse off after a couple of minutes. A mustard foot bath is also reputed to help relieve the problem of smelly feet.

ROAST VENISON WITH MUSTARD AND MUSHROOMS

Serves 4

600g (1lb 5oz) piece loin of venison,
    about 6.5cm (2½in) in diameter
1 level tbsp wholegrain mustard
2 small onions, thinly sliced
350g (12oz) small shiitake or brown-cap
    mushrooms
150ml (¼pint) olive oil
1tbsp freshly chopped thyme
1tbsp freshly chopped parsley
5tsp balsamic vinegar
Lemon juice, to taste

1 Preheat the oven to 230ºC (210ºC in a fan oven), mark 8. Rub the venison with the mustard and put it in a roasting tin. Scatter the onions and mushrooms around the meat and drizzle over half of the oil. Roast for 30–35min for medium-rare; 40min for well-done meat.

2 Remove the venison from the tin. Roll the hot venison in the chopped herbs to coat and put on a warmed serving platter with the mushrooms and onions. Cover with foil and leave to rest in a warm place while preparing the dressing.

3 Add the remaining oil and the vinegar to the juices in the roasting tin and warm on the hob, stirring. Season with salt and freshly ground black pepper and add lemon juice to taste.

4 Carve the venison into thick slices and serve with the hot dressing.

POT MARIGOLD

marigold and sage decoction

15g (½oz) fresh marigold flowers, or 5g (¼oz) dried flowers

15g (½oz) fresh sage leaves, or 5g (¼oz) dried leaves

1 Put the herbs in a pan, pour in 600ml (1pint) water and bring to the boil. Reduce the heat, cover with a tight-fitting lid and simmer for 10min.

2 Strain the liquid, pressing the herbs to extract all the liquid; discard the herbs. Allow the liquid to cool then pour into a bottle and seal with a tight-fitting lid. Store in a cool dark place for up to four days.

→ This is a useful gargle at the onset of a sore throat, but it tastes unpleasant. It can also help soothe itchy genital rashes if the whole amount is added to the bath. Omit the sage during pregnancy.

A cottage garden favourite, the pot marigold was once an important herb in daily medicinal and cosmetic use. It is indigenous to Asia and central and southern Europe but is easy to grow in cool temperate climates and is now cultivated worldwide. Its botanical name derives from the Latin *kalendae*, meaning 'first day of the month'; an allusion to its apparent ability to flower virtually throughout the year – certainly in warmer climates – or possibly to the fact that it is believed to regulate menstrual cycles. I once found a lone bloom in my garden on a mild winter day, proof of the plant's readiness to flower whenever beneficial conditions prevail. Its habit of opening and closing its petals with the sun was remarked upon by Shakespeare in *The Winter's Tale*: 'The marigold that goes to bed wi' th sun, And with him rises weeping.' Like seaweed, the dazzling orange bloom is also said to be a weather indicator – open flowers indicate a fine sunny day; closed flowers suggest rain.

The marigold is a hardy annual that grows 30cm (12in) high. It has tongue-shaped leaves and bears dazzling orange flowers throughout the summer.

Harvest flowers, just as they open or no later than mid-morning, throughout the summer for daily use fresh and for drying.

Take care not to confuse pot marigolds with other types of popular garden marigold. French, African and Mexican marigolds are all species of *Tagetes* and have entirely different properties.

Cultivation

Pot marigolds are the easiest of plants to grow. Simply sow seeds directly into the ground in early to mid-spring, choosing a sunny spot with a good and light but rich soil. Thin the seedlings to about 25cm (10in) apart. To extend the flowering season, deadhead regularly, but towards the end of the season leave a few blooms to form seeds – marigolds will self-seed freely given the right conditions. Pot marigolds will also grow happily in containers or window boxes.

Culinary use

The petals of pot marigolds have a mild, warm and faintly fragrant flavour, and can be used, fresh or dried, to flavour soups, casseroles, puddings, cakes and custards. They can also make an effective culinary dye. They can be used to replace saffron in recipes, but whilst the colour may be the same the flavour is somewhat different. Petals add an interesting zing to salads and omelettes and young leaves give a peppery flavour.

Medicinal use

The antibacterial, antifungal and antiseptic properties of pot marigold petals promote healing. They were used extensively during the American Civil War, when they were laid directly on wounds. Calendula cream is good for soothing raw, sore spots. As it does not sting, smells nice and is very gentle, it is especially useful for treating children's bangs and scrapes. Nursing mothers suffering with cracked and bleeding nipples will also find calendula cream soothing and healing; it is very safe, so it will not upset feeding babies.

A cold infusion of fresh marigold flowers can ease some of the symptoms of thrush. Use it as an eyewash to soothe conjunctivitis. Similarly, a compress or poultice of petals and leaves can relieve burns and stings. Many women assert that marigold has helped to ease painful periods and symptoms of the menopause.

Home and beauty

Marigold flowers make a cheerful potpourri, especially for a dark corner. Simply dry them on sheets of paper in an airy place out of direct sunlight.

HERB AND MARIGOLD PETAL PILAU

Serves 4

Petals from 4 marigold flowers
450ml (¾pint) hot vegetable stock
225g (8oz) basmati rice
40g (1½oz) butter
2 level tsp cumin seeds
4 cloves
7.5cm (3in) cinnamon stick
1 small onion, finely chopped
1 garlic clove, finely chopped
Leaves from 1 sprig of thyme
50g (2oz) raisins
1tsp runny honey
50g (2oz) shelled pistachio nuts

1 Put the petals from three of the marigolds into a small bowl and pour over the hot stock. Leave to infuse for 20min to draw out the colour from the petals.
2 Put the rice in a sieve and rinse under cold water until the water runs clear. Tip into a bowl and cover with 300ml (½pint) cold water and leave to soak for 7min.
3 Melt 25g (1oz) of the butter in a large, heavy-based pan. Add the cumin, cloves and cinnamon and cook for 1min. Add the onion, garlic and thyme leaves, stir everything together and cook gently for 5min until soft but not browned.
4 Drain the rice and add to the pan with the raisins. Cook for 1min, stirring, until the rice looks translucent. Add the marigold-infused stock, honey and ½tsp salt. Bring to the boil, stir once and cover with a well-fitting lid. Reduce the heat to low and leave to cook for 12min.
5 Meanwhile, quickly fry the pistachio nuts in the remaining butter until crisp and lightly golden. Gently fork the pistachio nuts into the rice and season well with salt and black pepper. Sprinkle over the remaining marigold petals and serve.

CARAWAY

We know that caraway has been used as a herb since the Stone Ages as its seed has been found among the remains of Neolithic meals as well as in Egyptian tombs. It is indigenous to India, North Africa, Asia, Europe and Siberia. It is mentioned in the Bible and its common name is believed to come from the Arabic *al-karwiya*, which means 'seeds'. The plant was also attributed with magical properties and believed to provide protection against witches and theft – any object containing caraway could not be stolen. For the same reasons it was often used in love potions.

Caraway formed the traditional finish to Elizabethan feasts, when a plate of seeds was served up with roast apples. It has long been a popular culinary herb in Germany and Austria, where it features in many traditional dishes, including sauerkraut. The essential oil is used to flavour the German liqueur known as *kümmel*. It found new favour in Britain after Queen Victoria married Prince Albert and caraway cake became a traditional teatime favourite.

This aromatic hardy biennial grows 60cm (2ft) high. It has feathery, bright green foliage and in its second year bears small clusters of white flowers from early to mid-summer, which are followed by the fruit that contain the seeds.

Harvest by cutting the brown seed heads in mid- to late summer, before the seeds begin to fall. Hang them upside down in a dry, well-ventilated room and tie a paper bag over each flower head or place a tray underneath to catch the seeds. Dig up the roots to cook and eat after harvesting the seeds.

Cultivation

Caraway is very easy to grow, but is best sown in autumn where it is to flower, in sun or partial shade. Thin the seedlings to 20cm (8in) apart upon germination. The plants will self-seed readily in the right conditions.

Culinary use

The seed has a warm, spicy, faintly liquorice flavour. It can be sprinkled over various rich meats to act as a digestive aid. The seeds can also be added to cabbage during cooking to reduce the nasty odour. Seeds can also be used to flavour cakes, biscuits, breads and soups and are delicious cooked with apples. Caraway comfits are simply the seeds crusted with white sugar. Caraway leaves can be chopped into salads and soups. The roots are also very tasty and can be boiled or roasted like parsnip.

Medicinal use

The seeds, roots and leaves of caraway have digestive properties similar to those of fennel, dill and anise. Simply chewing the seeds is supposed to ease indigestion and sweeten the breath. Caraway also soothes flatulence and helps ease colic in babies.

CARAWAY SEED CAKE

Serves 6
225g (8oz) butter
225g (8oz) golden caster sugar
4 large eggs
225g (8oz) plain flour
2 level tsp caraway seeds
1tsp vanilla extract

1 Preheat the oven to 180ºC (160º in a fan oven), mark 4. Grease a 20.5cm (8in) cake tin and line with baking parchment.
2 Cream the butter and sugar together until very light and fluffy. Beat in the eggs one at a time with 1tbsp of the flour. Stir in the caraway seeds and vanilla extract. With a large metal spoon, fold in the remaining flour and spoon into the cake tin, smoothing the top.
3 Bake in the oven for 1hr or until a skewer inserted in the centre comes out clean. Allow to cool slightly before turning out on to a wire rack to cool completely.

CHAMOMILE

chamomile tea

25g (1oz) fresh chamomile flowers,
or 15g (½oz) dried flowers

1 Pour 600ml (1pint) boiling water over
the flowers. Leave to infuse for 5min.
2 Strain the liquid and discard the
flowers before drinking.

rinse for fair hair

handful of fresh or dried chamomile
flowers

1 Put 1litre (1¾pints) water in a
pan and bring to the boil. Add the
chamomile flowers and leave to
infuse for 30min.
2 Strain the liquid, discard the flowers
and allow to cool before using.
➔ Use regularly to lighten blonde hair.

Although chamomile is a familiar herb, popular in herbal teas and known for its apple-like fragrance, it is not widely grown but deserves to be. It is indigenous to North Africa, parts of Asia and Europe. Its name is derived from the Greek *kamai*, meaning 'on the ground' and *melon*, which means 'apple' and alludes to the plant's fragrance. Chamomile is also known as the physician's plant because sickly plants often recover when it is planted nearby. The ancient Egyptians prized chamomile as a healing herb and it was much used as a strewing herb in the Middle Ages. For tea, German or wild chamomile (*Matricaria recutita*) is more commonly used as it is less bitter.

Chamomile is a low-growing perennial with tiny daisy-like flowers and feathery evergreen leaves, which form a glorious aromatic carpet.

When the plant is ready to harvest the flower petals will bend right back. Pick flowers to use immediately fresh or for drying.

Cultivation

Chamomile likes a dry, sunny position. Sow the seed in early spring where it is to grow; mix the seeds with sand to produce an even sowing. Keep the soil moist until leaves appear then thin the seedlings to 15cm (6in) apart. Chamomile will grow happily in containers, but it you want to harvest the flowers, a few pots probably won't supply a sufficient amount. This herb will self-seed freely given the right growing conditions.

The best variety to grow for a chamomile lawn is 'Treneague', which neither produces flowers nor requires mowing. Be prepared for the lawn to take time to establish – it cannot be walked on for 12 weeks after germination and preferably should be avoided wherever possible for its first year. Spraying the seedlings with an infusion of chamomile leaves and flowers can help prevent damping off disease. The same infusion will also help to activate the decomposition process in the compost heap.

Medicinal use

The aromatic oil in chamomile has antiseptic and anti-inflammatory properties. Infusions of the herb, taken as teas, have been shown to be helpful in soothing stomach ulcers, gastritis and upper respiratory tract infections, but need to be taken regularly – several times a day over a three-month period – before any improvements will be noted. As it promotes gastric secretions chamomile tea can be used as an aid to digestion. It is also a good gargle for relieving mouth ulcers. If you like the effect of chamomile tea but not the taste, add a slice of lemon and a teaspoon of honey. When in season, a large pinch of dried elderflowers also serves to sweeten the taste.

Use chamomile in the bath to soothe sunburn. Place a handful of flowers in a muslin bag and hang under the hot tap while running the water.

Home and beauty

A chamomile infusion makes an excellent rinse for fair hair; used regularly it will condition and lighten blonde hair. The same infusion can be used as a facial steam, but needs to be used hot. Used chamomile tea bags, left to cool then placed on the eyelids will reduce puffiness and tiredness. Chamomile flowers and leaves can be used in herbal pillows and potpourri.

CHICORY

Chicory is an interesting culinary herb to grow, although it does require a little care. The plant is unique in that it opens its flowers for precisely five hours a day and whilst the opening time will vary according to latitude, the leaves always align with North. This self-regulating habit is why chicory is often included in the style of the decorative bedding scheme known as a floral clock. The beautiful blue flowers are said to represent the eyes of a young girl weeping.

The ancient Egyptians, Greeks and Romans all used chicory as a medicinal and culinary herb, and during the Middle Ages it was commonly grown in kitchen gardens and used as a purgative. In the seventeenth century it was discovered that the roots made a bitter drink when ground to a powder. During both the First and Second World Wars the roasted roots were widely used as a substitute for coffee. In Europe chicory is often mixed with coffee in the belief that it counteracts the stimulant effect of the caffeine in the coffee.

Chicory is a tall, hardy perennial that grows 1m (3ft) high. It has long, hairy leaves and blue flowers that last from mid-summer to mid-autumn. Forcing the roots in warm, dark conditions produces the fresh, tasty new growth, or *chicons*, that is used in salads.

Chicons do not store well and quickly become limp so pick them as late as possible before use. Roots can be dug up throughout the summer until late autumn for eating, drying or forcing. Gather young leaves or flowers as required.

Cultivation

Chicory requires careful cultivation in two stages: the taproots must be produced in one year and then in the next they can be forced to produce the white heads of leaves, or *chicons*. The herb likes an open, sunny situation and well-cultivated soil. Sow seed directly into the ground in spring and for a good root harvest the soil must be well dug in advance and plenty of good farmyard manure incorporated into the soil.

If you want to cultivate *chicons* for use in salads, the variety 'Witloof', or Brussels chicory, is a good choice. Sow the seeds in early summer in drills then thin seedlings to 30cm (12in) apart. Keep the plants well watered if the weather is dry. Dig up the roots in late autumn, cut off the plant top above the root crown and replant, close together, in a box filled with good loam, with the crown flush with the surface. Water the roots then cover with a box or a pot so no light can get to the new growth. This will prevent the *chicons* becoming bitter. Keep the box in a minimum temperature of 10°C (50°F) for four to six weeks, when the *chicons* will be ready to harvest. The forcing process can be repeated but the second crop is never as good as the first. For a steady supply of *chicons*, store the roots after lifting in a fine soil-and-sand mix in a cool frost-free environment until required for forcing.

Culinary use

The *chicons* are usually used in salads, but are also delicious lightly fried. The flowers can be added to salads to give a dash of colour. The leaves can be eaten as a vegetable: boil for 15–20 minutes and serve with a *hollandaise* or *béchamel* sauce. Large mature roots can be used as a coffee substitute: wash the roots, then dry in gentle heat before roasting and grinding.

Medicinal use

Chicory leaves are used in poultices to soothe inflammation. It has been claimed that a decoction of the root may help to ease an inflammation of the urinary tract or the liver and may alleviate some of the discomfort associated with gallstones and kidney stones. Chicory acts as a mild diuretic, which helps the body to eliminate uric acid.

BRAISED CHICORY

Serves 4

700g (1½lb) chicory, trimmed and washed
25g (1oz) butter
¼ level tsp grated nutmeg
Juice of ½ lemon
150ml (¼pint) chicken stock
2 level tsp cornflour
2tbsp single cream
Freshly chopped parsley, to garnish

1 Blanch the chicory in boiling water for 1min. Drain, refresh in cold water, and drain again. Put the chicory heads in a single layer in a greased ovenproof dish and dot with the butter. Stir the nutmeg and lemon juice into the stock and pour over the chicory. Cover and cook in the oven at 170ºC (150ºC in a fan oven), mark 3 for 1½hr until the chicory is tender.

2 Mix the cornflour with 1tbsp water. Drain the juice from the dish into a small pan, add the cornflour mixture and season well with salt and freshly ground black pepper. Bring to the boil, stirring, and cook for 1min. Add the cream. Arrange the chicory in a warmed serving dish, pour over the sauce and sprinkle with chopped parsley.

CORIANDER

Coriander has been in use since ancient times. Seed has been found in ancient Egyptian tombs and the herb is mentioned in Sanskrit texts. In the Old Testament, the manna consumed by the children of Israel was likened to coriander seed, and coriander is one of the bitter herbs eaten at Passover as a reminder of the bitter and cruel way the Pharaoh treated the Jewish people when they were slaves in Egypt. The Chinese believed that coriander seeds conferred immortality on anyone who consumed them. In the Middle Ages the herb was regarded as an aphrodisiac and so was commonly included in love potions. The plant is indigenous to the Mediterranean region, but is now cultivated and used all over the world. The Romans, who used it as a preservative, flavouring and medicinal herb, introduced it to northern Europe and the explorer Christopher Columbus is thought to have taken it to the Caribbean from where its use spread to Latin America. The name is derived from the Greek *koros* meaning 'insect', probably because its curious smell is similar to that of the bedbug.

Coriander is a slender-stemmed hardy annual that grows 60cm (2ft) high. The leaf looks very like flat-leaf parsley, but has a distinctive and not altogether pleasant perfume all of its own. Flat clusters of tiny white flowers appear in early summer.

The leaves are best harvested before the plant flowers, after which the flavour deteriorates. Coriander leaves do not dry well, but freeze quite successfully. Collect seeds when the smell of the plant changes and becomes more pleasant. Place the flower heads in a paper bag and hang them upside down in small bunches, the seeds will drop or come away easily after about ten days. Store the seeds in an airtight container. Coriander roots are best dug up in the autumn.

Cultivation

Coriander enjoys a well-drained sunny site. It is fairly easy to grow, but hates damp or humid conditions. Sow seed in spring in shallow drills or pots, once all danger of frost has passed. It is best to sow coriander where it is to grow as it does not like being transplanted. For a leaf crop, space plants at 5cm (2in) intervals; for a seed crop, space them 23cm (9in) apart.

Culinary use

Leaves and seeds have pungent but different flavours. The sharp-tasting subtly perfumed leaves feature in many styles of regional cooking and are heavily used in South-East Asia. Coriander is a vital ingredient of *garam masala*, the Asian spice mix, guacamole and salsa. Add the leaves to soups, stews, curries and sauces. The spicy, aromatic seeds have long been used as a pickling spice. Add them to soups, sauces and vegetable dishes. The roots can be cooked as a vegetable or included in curries.

Medicinal use

Coriander combines the properties of a stimulant and a sedative, and it can become addictive if overused. The seeds are a digestive aid and act as a mild diuretic. A tea made from the seeds can be useful if taken before meals to stimulate the appetite and they will aid digestion and ease flatulence.

CORIANDER AND LENTIL SOUP

Serves 4

200g (7oz) red or puy lentils
1tbsp groundnut oil
1 large red onion, finely chopped
1 garlic clove, finely chopped
1litre (1¾pints) hot vegetable stock
2 carrots, peeled and chopped
1 celery stick, chopped
1 red pepper, deseeded and chopped
1 red chilli, deseeded and chopped
4 level tbsp freshly chopped coriander
4tsp single cream

1 Put the lentils in a bowl and cover with boiling water. Leave to soak for 1hr. Drain.
2 Heat the oil in a large pan and sauté the onion for about 10min until soft.
3 Add the garlic and cook for 1min, then add the stock, drained lentils, carrots, celery, pepper and chilli. Stir, bring to the boil, then simmer, covered, for 35min or until everything is tender. Season with salt and freshly ground black pepper. Leave to cool a little.
4 Whiz for 1–2min in a food processor with half the coriander. For a thicker texture, process only half the soup, leaving the other half chunky. Return to the pan, season and reheat. Serve in warmed bowls and garnish each bowl with the remaining coriander and a swirl of cream.

ROCKET

Rocket is a deservedly popular culinary herb. It is indigenous to the Mediterranean region and eastern Asia. The Romans used both the leaf and seed for culinary purposes, and it was a popular kitchen herb in Elizabethan times, eaten raw in salads as today. After the Great Fire of London in 1666, rocket was said to have grown over the ruins like a weed. It declined in popularity in Britain, but was rediscovered during the 1980s; in France, Italy and Turkey, however, it has always been prized. Its popularity over the last couple of decades has led to its being vetoed in the more fashionable restaurants as *passé*. This herb is so tasty, nutritious and easy to grow, however, that it deserves to be regarded as a classic herb and not subject to culinary trends.

If allowed to flower, this hardy annual can grow to 1m (3ft) in height. The elongated leaves are deeply divided. Rocket's distinctive creamy-yellow flowers bloom from summer to autumn.

Rocket is a cut-and-come again crop; picking encourages fresh growth and discourages flowering, after which the flavour of the leaves deteriorates. If you are harvesting rocket for medicinal purposes, however, pick the leaves when the plant is in flower. To ensure a constant supply of fresh leaves resow the crop at regular intervals throughout the summer.

Cultivation
In spite of the fact that rocket is expensive to buy it is very easy to grow. It prefers rich soil and light shade. Sow seed into the ground in spring when all danger of frost has passed and then water regularly – the leaves become bitter if not sufficiently hydrated. The leaves will be ready for harvesting within six to eight weeks of sowing. Although rocket can be cultivated in a pot, it does best in the garden.

Culinary use
The leaves have a sharp, peppery taste and are a wonderful addition to any salad, blending well with other types of salad leaf. The younger leaves have a milder flavour. Rocket is delicious even without a dressing or with just a light sprinkling of olive oil.

Medicinal use
Rich in minerals and vitamins, rocket is known to be helpful for preventing scurvy. It is sometimes used a tonic and a mild stimulant.

ROASTED MONKFISH TAILS WITH ROCKET PESTO

Serves 4

225g (8oz) shallots, peeled and halved

4 garlic cloves, unpeeled

2tbsp cider vinegar

2tbsp olive oil

900g (2lb) monkfish tail, skinned
    and filleted

4 sprigs of rosemary

4 sprigs of thyme

4 sprigs of oregano

For the rocket pesto

50g (2oz) rocket

15g (½oz) freshly grated Parmesan
    cheese

1tbsp olive oil

2tbsp apple juice

1 Preheat the oven to 220ºC (200ºC in a fan oven), mark 7. Put the shallots in a roasting tin with the garlic. Add the vinegar and oil and roast for 15–20min.

2 To make the pesto, put the rocket in a food processor. Add the Parmesan and oil. With the motor running, pour the apple juice through the feeder tube in a steady stream. Blend to a smooth paste.

3 Lay one monkfish fillet, cut side up, on a board and spread with the pesto. Put the other fillet on top, cut side down. Tie the two pieces together with string.

4 Remove the roasting tin from the oven, push the shallots and garlic to the sides and put the monkfish parcel in the centre of the tin. Season well and add the herb sprigs. Roast for 20–25min, until the monkfish turns opaque.

5 To serve, remove the string and lift the fish on to a serving platter, discarding any milky residue. Put the shallots and garlic around the fish. Serve with new potatoes.

MEADOWSWEET

meadowsweet infusion

15–25g (½–1oz) dried meadowsweet flowers

1 Put 900ml (1½pints) water in a pan and bring to the boil. Remove from the heat. Immerse the meadowsweet flowers in the hot water and leave to infuse for 10min. The water needs to be just off the boil, otherwise the steam will diffuse the salicylic acid and render the infusion less effective.

2 Strain the liquid and discard the meadowsweet flowers. Allow to cool before drinking.

➔ Drink up to 3–4 cups a day to control diarrhoea or ease the symptoms of colds and flu.

Meadowsweet is a sweetly scented plant that was once one of the most popular and commonly used herbs in Britain. Today it has been relegated to a merely decorative role – featuring in pondside and bog garden plantings, but it has much more to offer and deserves greater recognition.

In early times, the Druids regarded meadowsweet as a sacred plant. It became commonly used as a strewing herb because its aromatic perfume masked unpleasant odours. The Elizabethan herbalist Gerard maintained it was superior to all other strewing herbs for it pleased the senses without causing headaches, and it was reputed to be Queen Elizabeth I's favourite herb. It was much used in churches for strewing, particularly at weddings, and it was so commonly used in bridal bouquets that it acquired the popular name of bridewort. From the Middle Ages onwards meadowseet was used to flavour mead, the popular drink made from fermented honey. It was also frequently used to flavour beer and wine. The sap was the first discovered source of salicylic acid, a component required in the chemical production of acetylsalicylic acid, or aspirin.

Meadowsweet is native to Europe, Asia and China and grows in damp environments – marshes, swamps, fens, riversides and meadows. It is a tall, hardy perennial with aromatic foliage. The oval leaves have finely serrated edges and are a strong, dark green. The flowers are carried on tall, hollow stems that will reach up to 1.2m (4ft) in height. The creamy-white blooms form in beautiful clusters throughout summer and are exquisitely perfumed.

Pick the leaves for use fresh, or for drying, before the flowers appear. Gather the flowers for drying when new and fully open.

Cultivation

Meadowsweet likes partial shade and a fertile, moist alkaline soil. Sow in seed trays in autumn and leave to overwinter in a cold frame; try to ensure that the soil does not dry out. Germination will not take place until the spring. When the seedlings are large enough to handle, plant them out 30cm (12in) apart. Alternatively, sow seed in early spring, planting out into nursery beds when the seedlings are large enough to handle, ready for transplanting to their final positions in the autumn. The easiest method of propagation is to lift and divide established clumps in the autumn. Meadowsweet looks good in a container, but must be kept sufficiently moist.

Culinary use

The flowers have a faint almond flavour and can be added to jams and stewed fruits. They can also be used in home brewing and are said to make a delicious wine. Meadowsweet flower vinegar, which is easy to make, is delicious and makes a delightful contribution to summer salads.

Medicinal use

Meadowsweet is reputed to be helpful for treating colds and influenza, kidney and bladder complaints and rheumatism. It is also a traditional treatment for diarrhoea.

Home and beauty

Meadowsweet has a glorious fragrance and is superb in its purest form – picked as a bunch of flowers to scent a room. The dried flowers and leaves are wonderful ingredients for herb bags, which can be used to scent linen stored in drawers and cupboards. They also make a fragrant addition to potpourri.

FENNEL

Fennel is a glorious herb. Not only can every part of it be eaten, but it also has a delicate and uplifting aniseed fragrance, and its tall graceful beauty makes it an indispensable garden plant. In ancient times, both the Greeks and the Romans were enthusiastic consumers of fennel, using it as a slimming aid. Similarly the Anglo-Saxons took fennel on fasting days to help stave off hunger pangs. Roman soldiers also ate fennel to maintain good health. In the Middle Ages it was used regularly as a strewing herb to scent rooms and keep insects at bay.

Indigenous to Asia and the Mediterranean region, fennel is a striking hardy perennial that grows 1.5m (5ft) high. It is cloaked with delicate, bright green foliage and topped all summer long with yellow flowers in large umbels. Bronze fennel (*Foeniculum vulgare* 'Purpureum') has soft bronze-red foliage with darker sulphur-yellow flowers. Florence fennel (*F. vulgare* var. *dulce*) is a biennial grown as an annual for its bulbous base, which is a delicious, aniseed-flavoured vegetable. Fennel is a useful companion plant as it attracts hoverflies, which feed on whitefly.

Cut leaves and dig up roots in season as required. Seeds are ready to harvest when they become hard and turn a grey-green colour, usually in early autumn. To collect the seeds, cut off the flower heads and hang them upside down with a tray underneath to catch the seeds as they fall.

Cultivation

Fennel is a very easy herb to grow and given the right conditions will self-seed freely. It likes a sunny position in well-drained soil; if you garden on a heavy clay soil add some sand and gravel to improve drainage. Sow fennel seed directly into the ground after all danger of frost has passed, then thin the seedlings to 50cm (20in) apart. Fennel will grow happily in a container, but it may need staking when in flower. It will need repotting annually.

If you are growing Florence fennel for the bulbs, prepare the ground more thoroughly, digging in compost in the winter. Keep plants well watered and when the stem bases begin to swell draw the earth around them as you would for potatoes. Harvest the stem bulbs in late summer.

Fennel stems can be cut down and cleared away at the end of the summer. Alternatively, they can be left to provide strong architectural shapes through the winter, then be cut back in spring. Fennel is similar in appearance to dill, but the two plants should not be grown in close proximity as the seeds cross-pollinate.

Culinary use

Fennel's delicate aniseed flavour makes it a useful culinary herb and it is commonly associated with fish. The leaves can be used in marinades or stuffing for fatty meats such as pork or duck. Finely chopped fresh leaves are delicious sprinkled over boiled new potatoes. Fennel seeds have a stronger flavour than the leaves. The bulbs of Florence fennel can be cooked as any other root vegetable but are particularly delicious when roasted. They can also be eaten raw, grated into salads.

Medicinal use

Fennel is said to be a good aid to digestion and helpful in alleviating both heartburn and constipation. It also acts as a diuretic and is reputed to ease the symptoms of cystitis. A teaspoon of fennel tea is said to be good for babies with colic. If you cannot persuade a baby to take it, it may be equally helpful for the nursing mother to drink a little fennel tea instead. Drink fennel tea in moderation as consuming large quantities can cause convulsions and disturb the nervous system. An infusion of fennel seeds or leaves can be used as a soothing wash for tired and inflamed eyes. Chewing the seeds is said to reduce feelings of hunger, but they are no substitute for a healthy and balanced diet.

Home and beauty

Both seeds and leaves are said to have deep-cleansing properties so can be added to baths and facial steams. A facepack made from fennel tea and honey will soothe mature skin.

FENNEL, CHICORY, ORANGE AND HAZELNUT SALAD

Serves 10

600g (1lb 5oz) fennel bulbs, with fronds
500g (1lb 2oz) chicory heads or Chinese
    leaves, shredded
4 oranges, peeled and cut into rounds
50g (2oz) hazelnuts, chopped and toasted
Juice of 1 orange
4tbsp toasted hazelnut or walnut oil

1 Trim the fronds from the fennel, roughly chop them and put to one side. Finely slice the fennel bulb lengthways and put in a bowl together with the chicory heads (or Chinese leaves), orange slices and toasted hazelnuts.

2 Put the orange juice, hazelnut or walnut oil and reserved fennel fronds in a bowl, season well with salt and freshly ground black pepper and mix well. Pour over the salad and toss everything together.

WILD STRAWBERRY

The wild strawberry is not a hybrid of the fat modern fruit, but a plant in its own right, which grows naturally in Europe, Asia and North America. Its delicious fruit has long been appreciated – preserved strawberry seeds have been found in the settlements of prehistoric lake dwellers. The fruits were once associated with both Venus and the Virgin Mary and have been used as a symbol of righteousness. The botanical name is derived from the Latin *fragrans*, meaning 'fragrant', and refers to the wonderfully scented leaves, which smell of musk when dry. The plant's high iron, potassium and mineral salt content will be helpful to anyone suffering from anaemia. The leaves are also rich in vitamin C. The eighteenth-century Swedish botanist, Linnaeus, claimed that he cured himself of gout by restricting himself to a diet of wild strawberries for a short period of time.

This low-growing hardy perennial herb has deeply veined and serrated leaves. The pretty white flowers, which appear in late spring and continue into summer, are followed by the small red fruits in summer and autumn.

Pick leaves and fruit fresh as available. If required for drying, pick the leaves before flowering begins. Never use leaves that are only partly dried as a toxin is created during the drying process; when the leaf is completely dried the toxin disappears. The fruits freeze quite well.

Wild strawberries can cause an allergic reaction in some people.

Cultivation
The wild strawberry is very easy to grow. It tolerates sun or shade, but enjoys a sheltered position. The easiest method of propagation is by division as the plant spreads by sending out runners; separate daughter plants from the parent plant in spring. The seed is clearly visible on the surface of the fruit. To gather seed leave the fruit to shrivel and dry in the sun, then rub off the seed. Sow seed in spring and transplant the seedlings when large enough to handle. Plant at 30cm (12in) intervals. When the plants begin to fruit, feed them with a potash fertiliser.

Culinary use
Smaller and tarter than the commercially grown strawberry, the fruit of wild strawberries is delicious. It makes a wonderful jam, if enough fruit can be gathered. Alternatively, mix the strawberries into a fruit salad, or use to decorate a fruit flan. The most delicious cake I ever tasted was a tiny home-made cream puff, studded with wild strawberries.

Medicinal use
Wild strawberries are a diuretic, a laxative, a tonic and an astringent. They are helpful in treating anaemia, stomach upsets and nerves. Strawberry-leaf tea is said to be a good tonic for convalescents; it is not very tasty but can be mixed with other leaves, such as sweet woodruff, to improve the flavour. Put three or four leaves in a pot and pour over freshly boiled water. Include leaves or flowers of other herbs of your choice if you like.

Home and beauty
Strawberry juice added to a face-pack is said to whiten the skin and lighten freckles. Similarly, when applied to the teeth the juice will remove tartar and reduce staining. Leave the juice on the teeth for five minutes then rinse off with warm water to which a pinch of bicarbonate has been added. Cut strawberries applied to the skin are believed to soothe mild sunburn.

FRAGRANT RED FRUITS

Serves 6

450g (1lb) wild strawberries
225g (8oz) raspberries
125g (4oz) blueberries
125g (4oz) red or white currants
3 passion fruit
1 level tbsp golden caster sugar
2–3tbsp orange flower water

1 Put the strawberries in a serving dish with the raspberries, blueberries and red or white currants. Halve the passion fruit and scoop the pulp into the bowl.
2 Sprinkle the sugar and orange flower water over the fruits and toss together. Chill for at least 30min.
3 Serve the fruit salad with lightly whipped cream and dessert biscuits.

SWEET WOODRUFF

sweet woodruff tea

5g (¼oz) dried sweet woodruff
    leaves

1 Bring 600ml (1pint) water to the boil
in a pan. Remove from the heat and
add the dried leaves. Leave to infuse
for 5min.
2 Strain the liquid and discard the
leaves before drinking.
➜ Drink 1 cup at bedtime to help
induce sleep.

Although it may be small and insignificant, sweet woodruff is both a useful herb and a valuable garden plant. It is native to northern and central Europe, where it grows wild in woodlands. As it thrives in the dry shady conditions that many other garden plants will not tolerate, it is an ideal plant for growing under trees. It was commonly used as a fragrant strewing herb and for stuffing mattresses. The Georgians used to place leaf whorls in their pocket watches so that the aroma would be released whenever the watch was opened to check the time; they also used the leaves as naturally scented bookmarks.

Sweet woodruff grows to a maximum height of 30cm (12in) and is perfectly formed, with bright green leaves encircling the stem to make a delicate six-leafed ruff. Clusters of tiny, starry white flowers appear from late spring to early summer. The plants have very little perfume as they grow, but on drying the heady fragrance of newly mown hay combined with a dash of almond and vanilla intensifies.

Pick flowers and leaves for drying in early summer.

Cultivation

Sweet woodruff enjoys dry or moist shady conditions; its leaf colour will fade if it is planted in full sun. Given the right conditions it will offer excellent ground cover; indeed you may need to keep a check on its spread. The plant is easy to propagate. Just lift and divide clumps in spring, or take root cuttings in early summer after flowering. Only fresh seed will germinate so sow in seed trays in early autumn and then pot on or plant out after hardening off in spring.

Culinary use

Although it has no real culinary use, sweet woodruff is the basic flavouring of a traditional German drink known as May punch, which is delicious.

Medicinal use

Sweet woodruff is said to soothe stomach ache and act as a diuretic. It is also reputed to be helpful to anyone prone to gallstones. It is also a mild tranquilliser and an infusion of dried leaves will make a relaxing tea.

Home and beauty

To scent clothes and linen, and to deter moths, hang bunches of dried woodruff in wardrobes or place in drawers. You can also use sweet woodruff in herb bags or herb pillows. Try laying it under carpets, in the best tradition of a strewing herb.

MAY PUNCH

Makes 1.5–2.25litres (2$\frac{1}{2}$–3$\frac{3}{4}$pints)
Handful of fresh sweet woodruff leaves
Juice of 1 lemon
1–2 x 75cl bottles light white wine
    such as hock
4–6tbsp golden granulated sugar, to taste
75cl bottle champagne
3tbsp brandy (optional)
strawberries, hulled and sliced,
    for decorating
caster sugar, for sprinkling

1 Put the sweet woodruff leaves in an airing cupboard and leave to dry for 3 hr.
2 Put the dried woodruff leaves in a large bowl and pour over the lemon juice and 350ml (12fl oz) white wine. Leave to infuse for 3–4hr.
3 Pour over the remainder of the white wine and add 4–6 tbsp sugar to taste. Put in the fridge to chill.
4 When ready to serve, pour into a punch bowl and pour in the champagne and brandy, if using. Sprinkle a few sliced strawberries with caster sugar and add to the punch for decoration.

LIQUORICE

liquorice decoction

40–50g (1½–2oz) fresh or dried
  liquorice root

1 Put 900ml (1½pints) water in a pan
and bring to the boil. Add the liquorice
root and boil for 10–15min.
2 Strain the liquid and discard the root
before drinking.
➜ Drink 1 cup three times a day as
required to relieve coughs, colds, sore
throats and stomach ulcers. As this
herb can aggravate hypertension, blood
pressure should be monitored during
any long-term use.

Liquorice is popularly regarded as a confectionery rather than a herb, but in fact it is
the juice from the liquorice root that provides the famous flavouring used in sweets and
beer. The botanical name is derived from the Greek *glycyrriza*, meaning 'sweet root',
and *glabra*, meaning 'smooth'. The herb is indigenous to the area that stretches from
southern Europe to south-western Asia. The ancient Egyptians, Greeks and Romans
all recognised its soothing properties, using it to treat coughs and colds. Liquorice also
helps to prevent thirst; according to legend, Scythian warriors were able to last for ten
days without food or water merely by eating liquorice. It was introduced to England in
the sixteenth century where it became an important crop. The enormous cobbled
courtyard at Pontefract Castle was covered in topsoil so that the plant could be grown
and it is there that the famous Pontefract, or Pomfrey, cake was developed.

A hardy perennial, liquorice grows up to 1.5m (5ft) in height. It has narrow
opposing leaves and bluish-purple pea-like flowers, which appear in late summer. These
are followed by reddish-brown seed pods.

Roots can be harvested for drying when the plant is three or four years old.

Cultivation

Liquorice enjoys a deep, rich
moist soil and performs best in long, hot
summers. It is very difficult to grow from
seed, and root division is the most efficient form of propagation. Lift and divide
in autumn or spring, when the plant is
dormant; the pieces of root should contain a minimum of one bud. Place each
piece in a pot, cover with compost, water
and leave in a warm place until shoots
appear. Harden off the new plants before
planting out at 1m (3ft) intervals. The
plants take a couple of years to become
established, so be patient.

Culinary use

Liquorice root contains gly-
cyrrhiza, which is much sweeter than
sugar and is used as a flavouring in confectionery, beer and tobacco. Diabetics
can safely eat true liquorice sweets.

Medicinal use

Liquorice is a renowned remedy
for chest infections and colds and is still
widely used in commercial cough remedies and throat sweets. It also lowers
acidity levels in the stomach, helping
to relieve indigestion and heartburn.
Because liquorice spreads a protective
film over the stomach wall, it can help to
ease the pain caused by stomach ulcers.
Although it is reputed to help lower blood
cholesterol levels, prolonged use can
raise blood pressure. A decoction makes
an effective laxative for children. The
decoction is also helpful in treating
coughs, colds, sore throats and stomach
ulcers; drink as required.

WITCHHAZEL

witchhazel infusion

25g (1oz) witchhazel leaves, bark
   or twigs

1 Put 900ml (1½pints) water in a pan
and bring to the boil. Remove from the
heat and add the witchhazel. Leave to
infuse for 10min.

2 Strain the liquid and discard the
leaves, bark or twigs before drinking.

→ Drink the infusion to ease bowel
complaints. Be warned – it does not
taste very nice.

Gardeners value witchhazel for the strongly scented and striking autumn flowers, which are borne on bare boughs. But the plant is also widely known for the medicinal astringent that bears its name; the solution is a distilled extract from the young twigs. The shrub is native to North America, where native Americans have long used it as a compress to reduce painful swelling. Witchhazel possesses anti-inflammatory properties, tightens tissue and staunches the flow of bleed at the point of application. The herb's common name comes from its associations with witchcraft and the fact that its forked boughs were once used as divining rods to locate both water and gold.

A hardy deciduous shrub or small tree, witchhazel carries deeply veined elliptical leaves. Clusters of exotic, spider-like, four-petalled yellow flowers appear on the branches after the leaves have fallen and last through autumn. Their wonderful perfume will fill the garden on sunny winter days. The seed pods explode dramatically the following summer, firing seeds over some distance.

Gather twigs and leaves as required and crush to make infusions.

Cultivation
Occurring naturally in woodland, witchhazel enjoys sun and dappled shade and will tolerate moist or dry conditions. The best way to propagate it is by layering in autumn, but as a new plant will be slow growing allow plenty of time for it to develop before harvesting any twigs.

Medicinal use
Witchhazel is a powerful astringent. It can be used as a compress to soothe insect bites, burns, scalds, bruises and sprains. It is also helpful for treating bleeding noses and varicose veins. Cuts can be treated with diluted witchhazel. A diluted infusion can soothe the effects of diarrhoea, piles and other bowel complaints. For external use make a stronger decoction by doubling the amount of witchhazel to water.

Home and beauty
The astringent properties of witchhazel make it useful for closing pores and it makes an effective after-shave lotion.

HOP

The hop is a strikingly attractive herb that will scramble over, and cover, all manner of unsightly objects. According to first-century AD records, the Romans consumed hops as a vegetable and grew it extensively in their gardens. By the eighth century the herb's preserving and flavouring qualities had been discovered and it was widely used in Europe in the brewing industry. Eventually the herb was much used as an appetite stimulant, a mild painkiller and a sedative. Indigenous to northern temperate zones, hops are now grown commercially in northern Europe, North America and Chile.

Hop plants are vigorous hardy perennials with twining stems. The new shoots, which twist in a clockwise direction, can grow 7.5m (25ft) high before they die back completely in the autumn. The plant has attractive, deeply lobed leaves, reminiscent of the grapevine, and bears male and female flowers on different plants. The male flowers are small and green, the female flowers, the source of the hop's essential oils, are large and unmistakable. The fragrance they exude has been likened to the unlikely combination of yeast, garlic and ripening apples.

To harvest, pick side shoots in spring, the leaves as required and the flowers in early autumn. Collect stems in late autumn.

Cultivation

Hops are easy to grow as long as they are given good support. The gender of a plant is not clear for the first two to three years, but only female plants should be reproduced. The favoured forms of propagation are root division in spring or softwood cuttings in spring or early summer from established female plants. Seed must be fresh and is best obtained from a specialist supplier. It can be sown directly into the ground in spring and thinned to 30cm (12in) intervals. Thin out young shoots in the spring, but instead of throwing them away cook them as a vegetable. Spent hops that have been used for brewing make excellent garden mulch. Hops can be grown in containers, but require regular feeding throughout the summer and repotting each spring.

Culinary use

Young shoots are considered a great delicacy in parts of Italy, Belgium, Germany and France. They can be cooked like asparagus in lightly salted, boiling water and are delicious served with eggs, on toast or in a risotto. The male flowers can be parboiled, cooled and added to summer salads. The female flowers contain the resin that imparts the aromatic bitter taste and smell; when ripe and dried they are used to flavour, clear and preserve beer – but must be used within a few months of drying otherwise the flavour becomes unpleasant. Leaves can be added to soup, but should be blanched first to remove bitterness.

Medicinal use

The hop is both a sedative and a soporific, and it acts as a diuretic. Only female plants are used for medicinal purposes. An infusion of flowers makes a mild sedative tea, but you can add the flowers to any other herbal tea to make a digestive aid and appetite stimulant. Hops were traditionally reputed to help nursing mothers improve milk production, and recent research has shown that the herb contains a hormone that explains this therapeutic action.

Home and beauty

Hop pillows for inducing sleep are easy to make; dry the hop flowers, sprinkle with alcohol and place in a small cushion or pillowcase. In Kent hop stems are traditionally hung from kitchen ceilings and along the beams in pubs in the belief that they help to eliminate odours and discourage insects, but they must be renewed annually. The boughs must be hung green in autumn, while they are still flexible. Although they dry out rapidly, they retain the leaves and fruit.

HOP SHOOT OMELETTE WITH CREAM CHEESE AND CHIVES

Serves 1

3 medium eggs
25g (1oz) butter
25g (1oz) fresh hop shoots (the top
    5cm/2in only)
15g (½oz) cream cheese
1tsp freshly chopped chives

1 Beat the eggs in a bowl and season
with salt and freshly ground black pepper.
2 Melt half of the butter in a 15cm (6in)
non-stick or heavy-based frying pan.
When the butter is foaming, add the hop
shoots and toss over a high heat for a few
seconds to heat through. Season and tip
into a bowl.
3 Melt the rest of the butter in the same
frying pan, swirling it around so that it
coats the sides of the pan. When the
butter is foaming, pour in the eggs and
cook over a medium-high heat, drawing
the cooked egg in from the sides of the
pan and away from the base as it sets
with the back of a fork and allowing the
liquid egg to run underneath.
4 As soon as the omelette is set underneath but still slightly creamy on top,
spoon the hop shoots into the centre and
dot over the cream cheese. Sprinkle over
the chives. Flip one half of the omelette
over the shoots, then flip over the other
side and slide it out on to a warmed plate.
Serve immediately.

HYSSOP

hyssop tea

15g (¹/₂oz) dried hyssop flowers

1 Put 900ml (1½pints) water in a pan and bring to the boil. Remove from the heat and add the hyssop flowers. Leave to infuse for 10min.
2 Strain the liquid and discard the flowers before drinking.
→ Drink up to three small glasses a day for throat and bronchial complaints.

A pretty herb with a strong aromatic perfume, hyssop deserves to be more widely grown. It is indigenous to the Mediterranean region, where it grows wild on dry, rocky sites. It is mentioned several times in the Bible. The following verse, 'Purge me with hyssop, and I shall be clean: wash me, and I shall be whiter than snow' (Psalm 51 v.7), has prompted much debate as to whether or not this really referred to hyssop or another herb altogether, such as oregano or savory. However, as it has now been established that the penicillin-producing mould that grows on the leaves has some antibiotic effect, it is quite possible that hyssop could have been used in biblical times to offer a degree of antibiotic treatment in the bathing of lepers. Hyssop's strong flavour led to its use in preserving meat. In the first century AD, the Roman writer, Pliny, mentioned a wine called *hyssopites*, and hyssop is still used today to flavour liqueurs such as Chartreuse.

Hyssop is a hardy semi-evergreen shrub that can grow to 1.2m (4ft) if left unchecked. The narrow, pointed dark green leaves grow on erect stems and are aromatic. Blue, pink or white flowers are produced on spikes through summer. Hyssop attracts bees and is a useful companion plant for growing near cabbages as it tempts away cabbage whitefly.

Cut young leaves and flowers for drying in summer. The fragrance of the flowers improves with drying.

Cultivation

Hyssop enjoys a sunny position in well-drained soil. Sow seed directly into the ground in spring and thin seedlings to 30cm (12in) intervals. Hyssop can also be propagated by root division in spring or autumn, or by taking stem cuttings in spring. Like lavender, it can be used to edge herb or flower beds and can be clipped into shape, but it will need replacing every five years or so. Hyssop is a good container plant.

Culinary use

The herb has a pungent mint taste allied to a sharp bitterness. The leaves are particularly useful for flavouring soups, sauces and stuffing that will accompany rich game or fatty meat, as they will aid digestion at the same time. In Gascony, France, hyssop is used in *bouquet garni* while in North America it is sometimes used in fruit pies, the merest pinch being sprinkled over the fruit.

Medicinal use

Hyssop aids digestion. Almost one per cent of the hyssop plant consists of an essential oil whose medicinal action is similar to that of garden sage. Gargling with a warm infusion of the flowers is effective for sore throats. The herb is also helpful in treating bruising in general and a black eye in particular. Crush a handful of leaves in a muslin cloth or clean handkerchief, dip into boiling water and apply to the affected area as hot as the patient can tolerate. Continue this treatment until the swelling begins to subside. This regime can also help to alleviate rheumatic pain. Hyssop can also be useful in treating urinary tract infections. Pregnant women should not use the herb.

Home and beauty

Hyssop acts as an insect repellent so is a useful herb for protecting clothes from moths. Make up herb bags and hang in wardrobes or lay in drawers.

BACON, APPLE AND HYSSOP STUFFING

Serves 4–6

25g (1oz) butter

1 small onion, finely chopped

75g (3oz) celery, finely chopped

6 rashers of rindless streaky bacon,
    chopped

1 Cox's apple, peeled, cored and
    finely diced

75g (3oz) fresh white breadcrumbs

3tbsp freshly chopped hyssop

1 medium egg, beaten

1 Melt the butter in a frying pan, add the onion and fry gently for 5min until soft and lightly golden. Add the celery and bacon and cook until golden. Add the apple and fry for 1min.

2 Tip the mixture into a bowl and leave to cool. Stir in the breadcrumbs, hyssop and season with salt and freshly ground black pepper. Stir in enough egg to just bind the mixture together and use the stuffing as required with roasted game birds such as young pheasant.

JUNIPER

see page 46

Widely used as a culinary and medicinal herb, juniper has been cultivated for centuries. Although native to the Mediterranean, it is now widely grown throughout the world. It was commonly used as a strewing herb in the Middle Ages and during times of plague it was burnt in houses and on the streets to purify the air. The berries and the plant's essential oil are used in the brewing industry to flavour gin.

Juniper is an aromatic evergreen shrub or tree that can grow 8m (26ft) high. It has needle-like leaves and insignificant flowers in late spring or early summer. The male flowers resemble small catkins while the female flowers look like small berries. The berries themselves are found only on female plants and take up to three years to ripen, when they change from green to blackish-purple.

Harvest berries at the end of the summer, but make sure that they are ripe as a single bush will contain berries of varying degrees of ripeness. Spread the berries out on a metal tray to dry and turn them regularly so that they will shrivel satisfactorily.

barley and juniper decoction

4tbsp barley
4 juniper berries

1 Put the barley in a pan with the juniper berries and pour in 600–900ml (1–1½ pints) water. Bring to the boil and simmer gently, covered, for 20min.
2 Strain the liquid and discard the barley and berries. Allow to cool before drinking.
➜ Drink 1 cup, two or three times a day, to relieve cystitis.

Cultivation

Juniper enjoys an open position in good garden soil. Sow seed from ripe berries in spring in a cold frame, but do not plant out seedlings in the garden until they are one to two years old. Stem cuttings can be taken from new growth in spring or autumn and planted out the following season. To produce berries you will need both male and female plants growing in close proximity.

Culinary use

Juniper berries are usually used dried. Their flavour is delicious when cooked with rich meat such as venison, game and pork and they are good mixed into the stuffing for goose or duck. Adding a few juniper berries to the water when boiling cabbage transforms this often bland vegetable. In sauces and marinades four juniper berries can be used to replace one bay leaf.

Medicinal use

Juniper is a diuretic and helpful in treating urinary tract infections, indigestion and bronchial complaints. A decoction made with juniper and barley can help relieve the symptoms of cystitis if taken two to three times a day. Steam inhalations are said to be beneficial in treating coughs, colds and catarrh. Juniper should not be used long term as a treatment and people with kidney problems should avoid it. As some varieties have abortive properties pregnant women should not use it either. Baths, foot baths and hand baths can sometimes relieve the pain of arthritis and rheumatism. Add 1 tablespoon of reduced juniper decoction (*see page 46*) per 4.5litres (1gallon) of water and soak the affected part for 15 minutes. A bath would obviously dilute the effect but could still be helpful.

QUAIL COOKED WITH JUNIPER

Serves 4

125g (4oz) butter
8 quail
300ml (½pint) chicken stock
6 juniper berries
2tbsp gin or brandy
Bunch of watercress, to garnish

1 Melt the butter in a large pan and fry the birds until brown on all sides.

2 Sprinkle with 1tbsp salt. Cover the pan and cook over a moderate heat for about 20min. Or cook in the oven at 180ºC (160ºC in a fan oven), mark 4.

3 When the birds are nearly cooked, add the stock, juniper berries and gin or brandy. Continue to cook for 10min until the birds are tender.

4 To serve, put the birds in a warmed dish and pour the cooking liquid around them. Serve immediately, garnished with sprigs of watercress.

SWEET BAY

Sweet bay, or sweet laurel, is well known as a culinary herb with pungent aromatic leaves. It forms the central core of the classic *bouquet garni* herb mix, withstanding all regional variations. It has always grown wild in the Mediterranean region and is mentioned in the Bible. It was widely regarded as a symbol of good fortune and a protection against evil, disease and witchcraft. Legend held that the bay was sacred to the Greek god Apollo; his prophecies were communicated through his priestess at Delphi, who consumed a bay leaf before pronouncing the oracles. The ancient Greeks and Romans venerated the herb and crowned their triumphant warriors, athletes and learned poets with wreaths made from it as a mark of respect. The botanical name for bay comes from the Latin *laurus*, meaning 'laurel', and *nobilis*, meaning 'renowned', while the word 'laureate' means 'crowned with laurels'. The ancient tradition for associating bay with learning has survived in modern languages: the French word for examinations, *baccalaureate*, is derived from the Latin *bacca laureus*, meaning 'laurel berry'; and similarly the English term 'bachelor' is applied to academic achievement.

Bay is a large evergreen shrub or tall tree, which given its head, can reach 7m (23ft). It has glossy, dark green leaves and insignificant yellow flowers in early summer, which are followed by small black berries.

Pick leaves to use fresh as required or to dry.

Cultivation

Bay enjoys a sunny, sheltered spot. It is quite tender for its first few years of life and may require some protection. Its shallow roots make it vulnerable to frost damage and the leaves scorch in very cold weather and biting winds. Once established, however, it is quite a sturdy garden plant. It is not easy to propagate though. Layering in spring is probably the most efficient way of increasing stock. Cuttings can be taken in late summer, but they require a lot of patience and determination, as well as a heated propagator and good humidity. Sowing seed is also difficult as germination can take as long as six months. Fortunately for the faint-hearted, there is a ready supply of bay plants available from garden centres. Untrimmed bay can grow very straggly, but regular pruning controls the shape and encourages new growth. It is a good container plant and can be clipped into formal shapes such as pyramids and standards (*see pages 24–26*).

Culinary use

Along with parsley and thyme, bay is one of the essential ingredients of the classic *bouquet garni* herb mix (*see page 172*). Long slow cooking is the best way to extract the flavour of the leaves which can be used fresh or dry, although if you have a bush in the garden you will never need dry leaves in the kitchen. It is used to flavour stock, soup, sauces and casseroles. A leaf added to a rice pudding gives it a delicious taste.

Medicinal use

An infusion of the leaves is said to stimulate the appetite and aid digestion. This renowned culinary herb is very safe, but remember that all other laurels are poisonous.

Home and beauty

Placing a single bay leaf in a tin or jar of flour is supposed to deter weevils. A decoction added to bath water will relieve aching limbs.

TOMATO AND SWEET BAY PASTA SAUCE

Serves 4

1.4kg (3lb) vine-ripened tomatoes

4tbsp extra virgin olive oil

1 large garlic clove, thinly sliced

12 fresh bay leaves

25g (1oz) butter

1 Cut a cross in the top of each tomato, then put half in a large bowl. Cover with boiling water, leave for 1min, then plunge immediately into a bowl of cold water. Peel off the skins. Repeat with the remaining tomatoes.

2 Cut each tomato into quarters, remove and discard the core and seeds and roughly chop the flesh.

3 Heat the olive oil, garlic and bay leaves in a large, heavy-based pan and cook over a low heat for 1–2min. Add the chopped tomatoes, lower the heat and leave to simmer for 50–60min, stirring occasionally, until the sauce has reduced and thickened.

4 Remove the bay leaves, season the sauce with salt and freshly ground black pepper and stir in the butter. Serve hot with pasta and some finely grated Parmesan cheese.

LAVENDER

lavender water

1–2tsp vodka or ethyl alcohol
6 drops of lavender essential oil

1 Put the alcohol in a glass and add the essential oil. Mix well until the oil is dispersed.
2 Put 200ml (7fl oz) water into a spray bottle. Add the alcohol and oil mixture and shake vigorously.
→ Use the lavender water as required. If you prefer a stronger perfume, add more drops of oil to the alcohol.

lavender sugar

550g (1lb 2oz) golden caster sugar
125g (4oz) fresh lavender flowers, stripped from their stems

1 Put the sugar and flowers in a sealed container for 10 days.
2 Sift the sugar to remove the flowers and use straight away.

Lavender is one of the best-known herbs and for good reason; it looks great, it smells wonderful and it has a broad range of uses in the kitchen and home. It is indigenous to the Mediterranean region, and the Romans, who used it to perfume their baths, probably introduced it to Britain. Lavender's name is derived from the Latin *lavare*, meaning 'to wash'. It became a feature of English herb and knot gardens in the Middle Ages and the Tudor period, when it was also commonly used as a strewing herb to mask unpleasant household odours and to repel insects.

Lavender is a strong evergreen subshrub, producing young silver-grey growth that ripens to green as it matures; the aromatic purple flowers last throughout the summer. It thrives in warm, well-drained soils and grows to 1m (3ft) high. It can be clipped into neat domes or grown to form dense hedges that will swarm with bees throughout the summer. It also makes an ideal container plant for a sunny terrace, demanding little in the way of care and attention. The variety *L. angustifolia* 'Hidcote' is more compact in form than the species. French lavender (*L. stoechas*) is a rather tenderer species with distinctive tufty, dark purple flower spikes. Lavender becomes increasingly woody as it ages and is not likely to be very productive after ten years.

To harvest the flower spikes for drying, cut them just as the flowers are beginning to open, when they look like fat purple seeds.

Cultivation

Lavender prefers a sunny, well-drained site and fertile soil. Some species are frost hardy, but where winters are harsh grow plants in a container and move into a sheltered position. Lavenders require very little attention. Clip them into shape every spring, taking care not to cut into the old wood. Remove the flower heads in late summer and, if necessary, trim the bush into shape in early autumn, well before any frosts. Lavenders can be propagated from cuttings: softwood cuttings in spring, or semi-ripe cuttings in late summer or early autumn. Layering is another effective form of propagation, best tackled in the autumn. Space plants for hedges 23–30cm (9–12in) apart.

Culinary use

Because of lavender's cosmetic and perfumery associations, it is easy to forget that this aromatic plant is a useful culinary herb. It needs a light hand in the kitchen, however, for it has a strong flavour. New leaves are best for culinary purposes and these should be finely chopped before use. Traditionally, lavender was used to flavour shortbread, custards, jellies, ice cream and teas, but you can be more adventurous. When cooking lamb or fish, for instance, try frying a little lavender – flowers or leaves – with garlic, but strain the juice before serving and discard the herb. Dutch lavender (*Lavandula vera*) is reputed to be the best type to grow for culinary purposes.

Medicinal use

In addition to its distinctive fragrance, which is still widely used in perfumery and toiletries, lavender has both antiseptic and disinfectant qualities. The oil is soothing when applied to burns and stings; just sprinkle a drop or two on to cotton wool or muslin and smooth over the affected area. It is also said to be calming and restful. Six drops of oil added to a child's bedtime bath will work as a calmative whilst a drop of oil massaged into the temples will help ease a headache. The best lavender oils are made from distillations and are widely available in shops.

Home and beauty

Lavender has many uses in the home. Herb pillows are reputed to aid sleep, and for a fragrant and relaxing bath you can simply tie bunches of lavender under the running water. Lavender bags filled with dried flowers have long been used to keep clothing fresh and to deter moths; they are easy to make using just muslin. You can also give bed linen a hint of lavender fragrance by spraying it with lavender water as you iron.

LAVENDER
ICE CREAM

Serves 6–8

Flowers from 10–12 large sprigs of
    lavender, plus extra for to decorate
6 large egg yolks
500 g (1lb 2oz) lavender sugar
    (see opposite)
600 ml (1 pint) milk
284 ml whipping cream
1 tsp vanilla essence

1 Pick off the flowers from the stems,
removing any brown or green bits. Put
them in small sieve and rinse, then pat
dry with kitchen paper.
2 Put the eggs and sugar in a medium
heatproof bowl and beat together until
they are thick and creamy.
3 Put the milk, cream and vanilla essence
in the pan and heat gently, bringing to a
gentle simmer, stirring all the time. Pour
the hot milk over the egg mixture and
whisk to combine everything together.
4 Rinse the pan and fill with 2.5cm (1in)
water. Rest the bowl on top, making sure
the base does not touch the water. Cook
the mixture, over a medium-high heat,
stirring all the time until it is thick enough
to coat the back of the spoon.
5 Remove the custard from the heat and
stir in the flowers. Cool, then chill for 2hr
to allow the lavender to infuse the
custard. Strain the mixture through a
sieve to remove the excess flowers.
6 Churn in an ice-cream blender following the manufacturer's instructions.
7 Transfer to a freezerproof bowl, smooth
the top and cover with clingfilm or kitchen
foil. Freeze for up to three months. Soften
in the fridge for 20min before serving and
decorate with lavender flowers.

LOVAGE

Lovage is a tall handsome plant with a distinctive flavour similar to that of celery, but rather less subtle. Although native to the Mediterranean region, the herb is now naturalised across the temperate regions of the world. Both the ancient Greeks and the Romans used it for various purposes, including chewing the seeds as a digestive aid and to ease flatulence. Lovage appeared in medieval monastery gardens, where it was used for both culinary and medicinal purposes. The leaves have an antiseptic and deodorising effect on the skin, which is probably why footsore travellers in the Middle Ages often placed it in their shoes. Once thought to be an aphrodisiac, lovage was also used in love potions.

A tall, hardy herbaceous perennial, lovage will grow 2.1m (7ft) high in four years. It carries its aromatic toothed leaves on long stems. Greenish-yellow flowers appear in clusters in early to mid-summer. The plant dies down completely in winter.

Pick leaves as required to use fresh, freeze or dry before the plant has flowered. Pick young blanched stems in spring to cook as a vegetable. Gather seed heads as they start to turn brown; tie a paper bag over the heads and hang them upside down to dry. Roots can be dug up and dried when the plants are two or three seasons old.

Cultivation
Lovage enjoys a sunny spot but requires good moist garden soil. It is easy to propagate by division in spring when the leaves begin to show. Plant the root sections at 60cm (2ft) intervals at the back of the border. Sow ripe seeds in moist garden soil in a sunny spot and transfer seedlings to their permanent planting position in late autumn or early spring. Lovage can be grown in a container, but as it does grow tall it requires a substantial pot.

Culinary use
Lovage can be used like celery to enrich the flavour of stock, stew, soup and casseroles. It has a very strong flavour, like a blend of musky lemon with celery, so use it with a light hand. Young leaves and stems can be eaten as a vegetable; just cook them in lightly salted water until tender. Young stems can be candied like angelica and used to decorate pies and cakes. The seed can be sprinkled over home-made bread immediately before baking or added to boiled rice and mashed potato.

Medicinal use
Lovage helps ease digestive problems, stimulates the appetite and acts as a diuretic. Use infusions of lovage leaves, seed or root (*see page 46*). This herb should not be used by pregnant women or by anyone suffering from kidney problems.

Home and beauty
Lovage is reputed to have a cleansing and deodorising effect on the skin. You can either add a decoction to the bath water or just toss some fresh leaves into the bath.

LOVAGE AND BLUE CHEESE OMELETTE

Serves 2
4 medium eggs
2tsp freshly chopped lovage
75g (3oz) Blue Cheshire cheese
15g (½oz) butter
Lovage leaves, to garnish

1 Whisk together the eggs, lovage and 2tbsp water, and season well with salt and freshly ground black pepper. Coarsely grate the cheese, or cut it into thin slivers and set aside.

2 Heat the butter in a 20.5cm (8in) non-stick frying pan. When foaming, pour in the egg mixture.

3 Cook over a medium-high heat for a few minutes, drawing the back of a fork through the omelette as it cooks to allow the unset egg mixture to run through to the edges of the pan.

4 When the omelette is set underneath but still creamy on top, scatter the cheese over the surface of the omelette. Leave for a few moments until the cheese starts to melt, then fold the omelette into three.

5 To serve, cut the omelette in half and slide it on to two serving plates. Garnish with lovage leaves and serve with a crisp green salad.

CRAB APPLE

The crab or wild apple is the distant ancestor of today's cultivated apple. The fruit, although small, hard and sour, is full of distinctive flavour. The tree is indigenous to northern Europe and Western Asia and has been around for a long time. Pips have been found lodged in prehistoric cooking pots and the apple features conspicuously in the Bible. The plant's botanical name, *malus*, means 'malicious' or 'bad'. Once used as a hedgerow plant, the crab apple self-seeded freely, making it a common feature of the British countryside. Today, it is normally cultivated as an ornamental tree for its spring blossom and autumn fruit and leaf colour. However, to regard the flavourful fruits as mere ornaments is little short of a crime as they can be used to make the most delicious jellies, pickles and wine. The fruits were also much enjoyed in centuries past. Shakespeare celebrates them in *A Midsummer's Night Dream*, when Puck confesses: 'And sometimes lurk I in a gossip's bowl,/In very likeness of a roasted crab,/And when she drinks, against her lips I bob.'

The crab apple is a deciduous, occasionally thorny tree, which varies in size according to the variety, sometimes growing to 8m (26ft) high. The pink, white or red flowers, which appear in great profusion in late spring, are followed by conical orange or red fruits in early to mid-autumn. *Malus* 'John Downie', *M.* x *robusta* 'Red Sentinel' and *M.* 'Veitch's Scarlet' are all good reliable fruiting varieties. Most trees will yield an apple crop of around 9kg (20lb).

Cultivation

Crab apples enjoy a fertile well-drained soil. Plant the tree in autumn or winter with a good dressing of compost and stake it for a couple of years until it is well rooted. Ensure the plant is well watered the following spring. It does not require severe pruning, but will crop better if dead wood and crossed branches are removed so that the centre is open allowing light to penetrate and air to circulate freely.

Culinary use

The fruit produces the most delicious jellies with a unique flavour that no commercially prepared jams could ever equal. It has a unique delicacy and sharpness that will make teatime a truly special meal. Try roasting crab apples and serving them with a joint of meat. The fruit also makes great pickles and a potent home-made wine, the flavour of which is redolent of old country life.

Medicinal use

The pectin found in apples assists the elimination of toxins, stimulates digestion and helps to balance cholesterol levels. Crab apple is one of the original Bach flower remedies and its essence is thought to help alleviate feelings of self-hatred and uncleanness.

CRAB APPLE JELLY

Makes 2.3kg (5lb)

2.7kg (6lb) crab apples

Preserving or golden granulated sugar

1 Wash the fruit and cut into quarters. Put in a pan and add 1.7litres (3pints) water.
2 Bring to the boil and simmer for 1½hr or until the fruit is mashed. You may need to add a little more water during cooking.
3 Strain the fruit through a jelly cloth. Measure the extract and return to the pan with 450g (1lb) sugar for each 600ml (1pint) extract.
4 Heat gently, stirring to dissolve the sugar then bring to the boil and bubble until a jelly is obtained on testing. To test for a set: the jelly is ready when the temperature reaches 105ºC on a sugar thermometer, or when a spoonful of jelly placed on a chilled saucer wrinkles when you push your finger through. When setting point is reached, take the pan off the heat.
5 Remove any scum with a slotted spoon then pot the jelly in warmed sterilised jam jars and cover (*see page 145*). Use within six months.

LEMON BALM

Lemon balm is a pretty plant with a delicious soft lemon fragrance that has been used for culinary and medicinal purposes for centuries. Bees are very attracted to this herb, indeed the botanical name *Melissa* comes from the Greek word for 'bee'. The ancient Greeks believed that if you put sprigs of lemon balm in an empty hive it would attract a swarm of bees into it. The Romans introduced the herb to Britain and it soon became a feature in the apothecary garden. It was used to lift the spirits and relieve tension. It was also reputed to improve longevity. In the thirteenth century Prince Llewellyn of Glamorgan claimed he drank melissa tea every day of his life and, according to legend, he lived to be 108 years of age. The herb was commonly used as a strewing herb and its aromatic qualities were utilised by perfumiers.

This herb, which is indigenous to southern and central Europe, is a half-hardy perennial that can grow 75cm (2½ft) high. The light green leaves are veined and toothed and have a strong lemony fragrance. If the plant is grown in full sun and dry soil the leaves may turn yellow and the scent and flavour become rather harsh. The insignificant yellow flowers that appear throughout summer and into autumn will attract bees to the garden. The variegated variety, *M.* 'Aurea', and the golden leaf variety, *M.* 'All Gold', are pretty alternatives and are just as useful.

Although the fragrance and flavour of lemon balm leaves are at their best when the flowers appear, you can pick leaves at any time. The leaves can be dried.

Cultivation

Lemon balm will grow almost anywhere but it thrives in rich, moist soil in a sunny spot and its scent will be stronger if it can be grown in these ideal conditions. Sow seed in early spring under glass or in a propagator. When the seedlings are big enough to handle, plant them out at intervals of 45cm (18in). Softwood cuttings can be taken in late spring and early summer. Lemon balm is an easy plant to lift and divide. It can be an invasive plant so keep its growth in check by lifting and dividing as necessary. It is a good plant to grow in a pot as this keeps root growth in check. As the herb is only half-hardy, growing it in a container is also useful where winters are severe, as it can then be moved to a sheltered position.

Culinary use

The lemon flavour of this herb is very delicate so it can be used quite freely. It can even replace lemon rind or lemongrass in recipes. Use it to make stuffing for pork or lamb, or lay it over a chicken prior to roasting. The herb is also delicious in fruit drinks, ice cream and fruit salads.

Medicinal use

Lemon balm is reputed to ease headaches and tension as well as restore the memory. It has antispasmodic, soothing and sedative properties and is used in many herbal teas, notably those designed to induce sleep. For a relaxing night-time drink add one teaspoon of lemon balm and mint leaves to hot water. A cup of lemon balm tea after a meal acts as a digestive and can also ease flatulence. A tisane made with leaves and flowering tips has been claimed to promote longevity. Fresh leaves applied directly to insect bites will soothe the skin and dried leaves can be used in a poultice. The essential oil of lemon balm is used in aromatherapy to counteract insomnia, anxiety, depression and headaches. Trials are currently taking place in Germany to test the antiviral properties of the herb as a treatment for herpes simplex.

Home and beauty

Leaves added to bath water will act as a gentle calmative and lift the spirits. An infusion of lemon balm makes a good final rinse for greasy hair.

MINT

The unmistakable aroma and flavour of mint has been appreciated since ancient times. A native of the Mediterranean region, it has been found in Egyptian tombs dating from 1000BC and the Bible records that Pharisees were condemned for collecting tithes in mint and rue. The Romans introduced mint to the rest of Europe and it was taken to North America by early settlers. Today it is widely used to flavour sauces, liqueurs, medicines and confectionery. The fragrance is also utilised in the perfume and toiletries industry.

Mint is a hardy perennial with many different species and varieties. Spearmint, or garden mint (*M. spicata*), grows 60cm (2ft) tall, has bright green leaves and small white flowers in summer and is grown for culinary purposes. Apple mint (*M. suaveolens*) has green and white variegated leaves and a wonderful apple and mint flavour. Pineapple mint (*M. suaveolens* 'Variegata') has slightly hairy green and cream leaves; although it smells delightful it is not suitable for kitchen use. Eau de cologne mint (*M. x piperata* f. *citrata*) has rounded green leaves, tinged with purple, which release a glorious smell; it is best used for fragrance and cosmetic purposes. Peppermint (*M. x piperata*) has medicinal properties: black peppermint (*M. x piperata* f. *rubescens*) and white peppermint (*M. x piperata* f. *pallescens*) are the most highly regarded varieties. Mint is a useful companion plant – spearmint or peppermint planted near roses will deter aphids.

To use the leaves fresh pick them as required. For freezing or drying, pick the leaves before flowering begins.

peppermint tisane

2–3tsp fresh mint leaves, or
1 level tsp dried leaves

1 Bring 150ml (¼pint) water to the boil and pour over the leaves. Allow to stand for 3–8min. A longer infusion will intensify the flavour.
2 Strain the liquid and discard the mint before drinking.

mint julep cocktail

1tsp caster sugar
2 sprigs of fresh mint
Soda water
3tbsp bourbon, or to taste

1 Put the sugar with 1 sprig of mint and a little soda water in a tumbler and mash to release the mint flavour.
2 Remove and discard the mint. Pour in the bourbon and more soda water to taste. Decorate with a sprig of mint.

Cultivation

Mint is fantastically easy to grow, so much so that checking its spread is usually more of an issue than getting it to grow. It likes moist soil in partial shade. The easiest method of propagation is by cuttings or root division in late winter or early spring. Mint is an ideal herb for growing in a pot, indeed it is generally recommended as the best method of containing its spreading habit. If you want to grow mint in the garden, sinking a pot in the soil and planting in that is an excellent way of controlling the roots.

Culinary use

Mints used in the kitchen are hybrids of wild species and all varieties freely hybridise with each other, inheriting different characteristics from their ancestors, which explains the range of flavours among the different mints. Spearmint (also known as garden or common mint) and Moroccan mint in particular have an excellent flavour. Mint combines well with tomatoes, cucumber and yogurt, it can be used in cold soups and it is an important ingredient in Middle Eastern dishes. It is famously added to new potatoes, either in the cooking process or finely chopped and sprinkled over prior to serving. Mint sauce and roast lamb is a traditional British Sunday lunchtime combination. Mint also has many uses in confectionery and desserts.

Medicinal use

Mint is antispasmodic, anti-inflammatory and antibacterial. It is commonly used as a digestive aid and for soothing headaches. Spearmint and peppermint are the mint species commonly used for medicinal purposes. Mint oils should not be used on or around babies. Pennyroyal mint (*Mentha pulegium*) should not be taken during pregnancy; the oil is an abortive and highly toxic and known to cause liver damage.

Home and beauty

Fresh leaves are said to heal skin blemishes and act as an astringent. Make a mint infusion, leave it to cool then dab on to the skin. For an invigorating bath, add fresh leaves to the water.

TABBOULEH

Serves 6–8

225g (8oz) bulgar wheat

4 spring onions, finely chopped

1 large bunch of fresh parsley, around
125g (4oz), roughly chopped

3 large sprigs of mint, roughly chopped,
plus extra to garnish

4 tbsp olive oil

Grated rind and juice of 1½ lemons

1 lemon, cut into wedges, to serve

1 Put the bulgar wheat in a bowl and add enough cold water to cover it by about 2.5cm (1in). Soak for 30min. Drain well in a sieve, put in a clean tea towel, wrap up and squeeze dry.

2 Mix the bulgar, onion, parsley and mint together in a bowl. Add the olive oil, lemon rind and juice and season well to taste with salt and freshly ground black pepper. Garnish with lemon wedges and sprigs of mint and serve.

BERGAMOT

bergamot tea

15g (1/2oz) fresh bergamot leaves

1 Bring 600ml (1pint) of water to the boil then pour over the leaves and leave to infuse for 5min.
2 Strain the liquid and discard the leaves before drinking.
➔ Bergamot tea is said to relieve symptoms of nausea and vomiting and is a mild soporific.

Bergamot is a strikingly attractive herb with deliciously aromatic leaves and exotic, spidery, many-petalled flowers. The plant is named after the sixteenth-century botanist and physician, Nicholas de Monardes, who was the first person to celebrate its properties. The smell from its crushed leaves closely resembles that of the fragrant plant *Citrus bergamia,* or bergamot orange, whose oil is used in the perfume industry, hence the herb's common name. Bergamot is indigenous to North America and grows around the Oswego River near Lake Ontario. The native Americans who lived in the region used it to treat chest complaints and made a tea with the leaves, which contain the strong antiseptic thymol. After the Boston Tea Party incident interrupted supplies of traditional Indian tea, many Americans began to drink bergamot tea, which became known as Oswego tea. The flavour is reminiscent of fragrant china tea, which made it an acceptable substitute for Indian tea.

A hardy perennial, bergamot grows 75cm (2½ft) high. It has toothed leaves and bears red or pink fragrant flowers with petals arranged in whorls throughout summer. The nectar-filled flowers are highly attractive to bees. *Monarda didyma* is the best-known bergamot species, but *M. fistulosa* and *M. citriodora* can also be used.

Use the leaves fresh as required or pick them before flowering commences for drying. Cut flowers for drying as they open.

Cultivation

Bergamot enjoys moist, rich garden soil in a semi-shady spot. Sow seeds in spring under cover. Harden off and plant out when large enough to handle at 45cm (18in) intervals. Named varieties will not grow true from collected seed, so to increase existing stock you will need to take cuttings from young shoots in early summer or propagate by division in early spring.

Culinary use

Leaves and flower petals have an extraordinarily rich perfumed flavour with a sharp citrus overtone. Fresh and dried leaves can be used to make tea and both chopped leaves and petals can be added sparingly to salads; too much herb will overpower the flavour of other leaves.

Medicinal use

A tea made with bergamot leaves will soothe an upset stomach and relieve menstrual pain. It is also said to be helpful with nausea and vomiting and is a mild soporific. An inhalation of the vapour from an infusion will relieve bronchial complaints and catarrh. Put a handful of leaves into a bowl, pour over boiling water and breathe deeply.

SWEET CICELY

Sweet cicely is a pretty herb that deserves a place in any herb garden for its looks alone. It resembles cow parsley, but is more delicate in appearance and the leaves have a delicious aniseed scent, to which both the botanical name (*odorata*) and common name allude. It is indigenous to western Europe and can be found growing wild in woods and hedgerows. Although it has now fallen out of culinary favour for no good reason, the herb has many culinary uses and all parts were consumed with relish down the centuries. During the sixteenth and seventeenth centuries, the seeds were made into a polish to give furniture a glossy finish and a wonderful smell.

A hardy perennial, sweet cicely can grow 90cm (3ft) high. It has stout hollow stems with delicate fern-like leaves and tiny white flowers, which are carried in loose clusters from late spring to early summer.

Pick leaves fresh as required. Gather unripe seed as required when green, or for storing leave them to fully ripen and turn dark brown in colour. Roots can be dug up in autumn for drying.

Cultivation

Sweet cicely enjoys rich, well-draining soil and light shade. Sow seed in autumn and leave in a cold frame to over-winter (it needs several months of low temperatures before it will germinate), but when germination occurs move the seed to a cold greenhouse. Plant out at 60cm (2ft) intervals when the seedlings are large enough to handle and all danger of frost has passed. Root cuttings can be taken in spring or autumn, alternatively the plant can be propagated by division in autumn after the top growth has died back. Sweet cicely self-seeds freely given the right growing conditions.

Culinary use

Both ripe and unripe seeds have a sweet, though different flavour (ripe has a hint more aniseed flavour than unripe), and can be used in desserts. The leaves have a mild aniseed taste and are delicious chopped and added to omelettes or mixed into salads. The leaves are also natural sweeteners; they can be used when cooking fruit to reduce the amount of sugar required. The fresh root has a faint aniseed flavour and can be cooked as a vegetable or used raw in salads.

Medicinal use

Sweet cicely is a very gentle herb. As the leaves can be used as a sweetener in cooking, this can be particularly useful for diabetics. The whole plant serves as a digestive aid and infusions of the root produce a mild tonic. The seeds can be chewed to relieve flatulence.

Home and beauty

The crushed seeds can be mixed with oil to make fragrant furniture polish.

MYRTLE

myrtle tea

5g (¼oz) fresh myrtle leaves
Honey, to taste

1 Bring 600ml (1pint) water to the boil.
Pour over the myrtle leaves and leave
to infuse for 5min.
2 Strain the liquid and discard the
leaves. Sweeten with honey to taste.
➔ Drink 1 cup up to three times a
day to aid digestion and ease chest
complaints.

Myrtle is an intensely fragrant herb. The ancient Greeks and Romans prized it. They also regarded it as the sacred herb of their respective love goddesses – Aphrodite and Venus – so planted it around their temples. According to legend, Venus was carrying a sprig of myrtle as she rose from the sea, as illustrated in Botticelli's *Birth of Venus*, and indeed the plant does grow well in salt air. Subsequently, the herb has been regarded as a symbol of love and was commonly used in bridal bouquets. An astringent dusting powder was once made from the leaves as an early form of talcum powder for babies, while the berries were used to make hair dye.

A half-hardy evergreen shrub, myrtle can grow to 5m (16½ft) if left unchecked. The glossy, dark green leaves are intensely aromatic, as are the white flowers, which appear at the end of spring and throughout summer. Purplish-black berries follow.

Pick the leaves for use fresh or to dry. Pick flowers for drying as they open. The berries can be dried; store them in an airtight container.

Cultivation

Myrtle enjoys well-drained soil in a sunny spot, but requires protection from frost and biting winds. It does best planted against a south-facing wall. Propagation can be by layering in mid-summer; when rooting has occurred, separate the new plant from the parent. Alternatively, take softwood cuttings in spring or semi-hardwood cuttings in summer. Young plants do best if maintained in pots for the first few years of life. Trim the shrub into shape in spring when all danger of frost has passed.

Culinary use

Myrtle berries have a somewhat bitter but perfumed flavour that is similar to juniper berries, and like them they can be crushed to flavour rich meat, such as venison, game and goose.

Medicinal use

The leaves contain a substance that has antibiotic properties; they are also antiseptic and astringent. Myrtle tea acts as a soothing expectorant and so is reputed to be helpful in treating chest complaints. It also relieves flatulence. A compress is helpful for treating bruises. Chewing the berries freshens the breath.

Home and beauty

Myrtle leaves and flowers are intensely aromatic and make wonderful potpourri and herb pillows. A decoction of the berries is said to be a good rinse for dark hair.

CATMINT

catmint infusion

15g (½oz) catmint leaves or flowering tips

1 Bring 600ml (1pint) water to the boil. Pour over the catmint and leave to infuse for 5min.
2 Strain the liquid and discard the leaves before drinking.
→ Children may have just 2–3 teaspoons several times a day (see below).

Catmint, or catnip, is a lovely herb with velvety grey leaves and delicate purple flowers that bloom all summer long. The wonderfully aromatic foliage and long flowering period have ensured its popularity as a garden plant. Indigenous to Europe and parts of Asia, catmint may have originated from the Roman town of Nepeti, where it was reputed to have grown freely. The herb was formerly used as a seasoning and the leaves, which are mildly hallucinogenic, were smoked. As the common name suggests the fragrance is that of a musky mint. Apparently this aroma is similar to feline pheromones, which explains why cats are so drawn to the plant. Drawn is perhaps an understatement; cats love this herb so much that their ecstatic rolling about on it can sometimes kill it. One solution to the problem is to grow several plants so that the local cat, or cats, does not concentrate its attentions on a single plant.

A hardy herbaceous perennial, catmint throws up a mass of stems each spring that can grow to 50cm (20in) high. The grey leaves are borne in whorls and the violet or blue flowers appear at the top of the stems from mid-summer through to early autumn. There are many different species and varieties of catmint: *N. cataria* is the true herb for medicinal and culinary use. *N. x faassenii* 'Six Hills Giant' is a vigorous and pretty plant for garden cultivation.

Pick leaves and flowers to use fresh or for drying when young.

Cultivation

Catmint enjoys a well-drained site in sun or light shade. Sow seed directly into the ground in spring or late summer or into seed trays in spring if preferred. Plant out when large enough to handle, or thin to 30cm (12in) intervals. This is an easy plant to propagate by division and softwood cuttings can be taken in spring or early summer before flowering commences. When the herb has finished its first flush of flowering cut it back hard and it will repeat the performance. Catmint is a good container plant.

Medicinal use

The plant has little modern medicinal use although it is thought to be soothing to children suffering from infectious diseases, as it is a mild sedative; it induces sleep and increases perspiration without raising body temperature. *N. cataria* is the only catmint that can be used for medicinal purposes.

Home and beauty

You can use catmint to make desirable toys for your cats. Crumble dried leaves, stuff them into a fabric envelope and sew up securely. Cats especially love these toys if they are constructed with fluffy or furry material – feathers sewn on are an added bonus. Rats are said to hate the smell, so strew the herb around liberally if you suspect you have a problem.

BASIL

basil infusion

5–15g (¼–½oz) fresh basil leaves

1 Put 900ml (1½pints) water in a pan and bring to the boil. Remove from the heat. Add the basil and leave to infuse for 5min.
2 Strain the liquid and discard the basil before drinking.
➔ Drink 1 cup up to up to three times a day.

Basil, also called sweet basil, is an essential herb in the contemporary cook's kitchen. The plant is indigenous to the area between the Middle East and India, but has been cultivated in the Mediterranean region for thousands of years. The Hindus regarded it as a sacred herb and used it to disinfect homes affected by malaria. It was supposed to have grown around Christ's tomb after the resurrection, and the common name, basil, is thought to derive from the Greek *basilicon phuton,* which means 'kingly herb'. In some Greek Orthodox churches pots of basil are still placed under the altar. The herb has a mixed reputation, however. In ancient Greece and Rome, where it was associated with poverty and misfortune, legend records that seed had to be cursed as it was sown to ensure its germination. Equally, its reputation as a medicine was varied, with some herbalists believing it to be uplifting to the spirit and others insisting it was poisonous – principally because it will not grow in close proximity to the herb rue.

A low-growing tender annual or short-lived perennial, basil grows 50cm (20in) high. It has fragrant, shiny green oval leaves, with clear veining. Purple basil (*O. basilicum* var. *purpurascens*) has the same aromatic properties, but boasts deep purple leaves. Bush basil (*O. minimum*) grows a mere 15cm (6in) high and has smaller leaves.

To harvest, pick young leaves from the top of the plant to promote plenty of bushy growth. Basil is not the easiest herb to dry successfully so it is better to make herb oil or vinegar using fresh leaves, for use later in autumn and winter. Basil can be frozen and having a supply stored in the freezer for use in an emergency is always helpful.

Cultivation

Basil likes warmth, so for best results grow this herb in a sheltered, sunny spot in well-drained fertile soil. It is usually grown as an annual from seed. Sow seed in early spring in pots under glass, or directly into the ground in late spring or early summer after all danger of frost has passed. For an early crop sow the seeds in a warm greenhouse. Basil does not transplant easily so it is safest to put just a few seeds in a single pot. Harden off the plants just before they are ready to plant out. When the plants are established pinch out the growing tips to encourage bushy growth. Basil needs to be well watered, but take great care not to over water because it is susceptible to damping off disease, particularly if seed trays or pots are overcrowded. This herb makes a useful and productive container plant.

Culinary use

This popular culinary herb mixes particularly well with tomatoes and eggs. It is a pivotal herb in many pasta dishes and notably *pesto*. Its flavour intensifies with cooking, so it should be added to sauces at the last moment. It tastes better torn rather than chopped. The leaves can be mixed into salads or used to make flavoured oil or vinegar, both of which are perfect for salad dressings.

Medicinal use

Basil is said to have sedative and antispasmodic properties, which make it helpful for easing nervous disorders, migraines, headaches and colic in children. Infusions drunk two to three times a day may be therapeutic.

PESTO

Makes about 300 ml (½pint)
50g (2oz) fresh basil leaves
2 garlic cloves
2tbsp pine nuts
50g (2oz) freshly grated Parmesan
   cheese
125ml (4fl oz) olive oil

1 Grind the basil, garlic and pine nuts to a paste using a pestle and mortar. Season well with salt and black pepper.
2 Add the Parmesan cheese and blend well. Transfer to a bowl and beat in the oil, a little at a time, stirring vigorously with a wooden spoon. Serve cold, with freshly cooked pasta.

Variation
To make the pesto in a blender or food processor, put the basil, garlic, pine nuts and olive oil in the blender or food processor and whiz until very creamy. Transfer the mixture to a bowl, fold in the cheese and mix thoroughly. Season well.
   Store the sauce for up to two weeks in a screw-topped jar in the fridge.

EVENING PRIMROSE

As its name suggests, evening primrose opens its flowers in the evening, at least early on in the season. It is indigenous to North America, where native Americans ate the stems and leaves as food. The plant has astringent and soporific properties and the seeds are rich in gamma-linoleic acid, which is used by the body to produce prostaglandins, which in turn help maintain healthy body tissue and restrict inflammatory reactions. The botanical name for evening primrose is derived from the Greek *oinos*, which means 'wine', and *thera*, which means 'hunt'. True to its name, the herb used to be regarded as a treatment for hangovers and alcohol poisoning – a theory that is currently undergoing further scientific research.

Evening primrose is a hardy biennial that can grow 1.2m (4ft) high. The leaves are long and lance shaped. The fragrant yellow flowers are borne at the end of the stems throughout summer. They emit a phosphorescent light, which makes them appear to shine out of the twilight.

Pick leaves to use fresh as required; they are best before flowering commences. Pick flowers to use fresh.

Cultivation

Evening primrose is very easy to grow and will self-seed freely given the right conditions. Although it will tolerate all kinds of situations, it prefers well-drained soil and a sunny position. Sow seed directly into the ground. When the seedlings are large enough to handle, transplant or thin to 30cm (12in) apart. Transplanting can encourage this biennial to flower in its first season. Alternatively, sow into seed trays and plant out when large enough.

Culinary use

Although in theory all parts of the evening primrose are edible – leaves, buds and flowers as well as the root – it is not widely consumed. Many people find the rough texture of the leaves unpleasant. The root can be boiled like other root vegetables and tastes rather like parsnip.

Medicinal use

Evening primrose has many medicinal properties and is the subject of much current research and interest. Its ability to relieve the symptoms of premenstrual tension is well known, and it has been shown to be beneficial in the treatment of eczema, arthritis, brittle nails, cramp and coughing. Claims that it can benefit sufferers of multiple sclerosis, help prevent heart disease and act as an aid for losing weight are all under current investigation. The seeds are the source of the essential oil, while the leaves and roots are used in infusions.

Home and beauty

The flowers can be used to make a facemask. They can also be infused in a bowl of boiling water to produce an astringent facial steam.

MARJORAM

There are three forms of marjoram, each with a distinctive flavour and use of its own: sweet marjoram (*Origanum marjorana*), pot marjoram (*O. onites*) and wild marjoram (*O. vulgare*), also known as oregano. Indigenous to the Mediterranean region, the herb is now cultivated worldwide. The botanical name is derived from the Greek *oros*, meaning 'mountain' and *ganos*, meaning 'joy', and reminds us that the herb grows freely on the sunny hillsides of Greece, filling the air with fragrance. It attracts bees and butterflies. Marjoram was thought to bring peace to the dead and was often planted on tombs. It was also thought to be an antidote to poisoning after Aristotle reported that if a tortoise swallowed a snake it would immediately eat marjoram to prevent it from dying. The Romans used the herb as a symbol of happiness and fashioned it into crowning wreaths for brides and grooms. The ancient Egyptians used marjoram as a disinfectant and preservative and in the Middle Ages wild marjoram, which contains the antiseptic thymol, was used as a strewing herb.

Sweet marjoram is a half-hardy, compact bushy plant, which is best treated as an annual. It grows to around 20cm (8in) and has small leaves and tiny white flowers. Pot marjoram is a small hardy perennial, which grows 45cm (18in) high. It forms a green mat in winter and carries pink flowers throughout the summer. Wild marjoram is also a hardy perennial and grows 45cm (18in) high. The hairy green leaves remain throughout the year and purple flowers appear in summer.

Pick the leaves to use fresh as required when they are in season. Freeze or dry them for use out of season.

Cultivation

All marjorams enjoy a rich, well-drained soil in a sunny situation. Sweet marjoram is best sown in early spring in a seed tray under glass. The seed is very fine and it can help to mix it with sand. Plant out in early summer. Pot marjoram can be propagated by softwood cuttings taken in spring or by division in spring or autumn. Wild marjoram is easy to grow from seed or can be propagated by root division in spring or autumn. Marjoram is a good container plant.

Culinary use

Sweet marjoram is the best culinary herb, being both spicy and sweet but not overpoweringly so. Pot marjoram has a more intense flavour and cannot be used with subtly flavoured food or it will overpower all other flavours. Wild marjoram, or oregano as it is often and confusingly known, is the strongest in flavour and is used in Italian cuisine for robust tomato sauces and pizza. Both pot marjoram and wild marjoram can withstand long cooking, but sweet marjoram is best added late in the cooking process. All three herbs are used to flavour pasta, tomato dishes and sausages.

Medicinal use

Marjoram has strong sedative properties and must be treated with respect. Mild teas can be a helpful soporific and sedative. The herb also soothes the digestive system and works as a diuretic and a tonic. It can be helpful in dealing with chest complaints due to its antiseptic properties.

Home and beauty

Marjoram makes a fragrant herb pillow. An infusion added to bath water is very relaxing.

NEAPOLITAN PIZZA

Serves 4

225g (8oz) strong white bread flour,
  sifted, plus extra for dusting
7g (¼oz) sachet easy-blend yeast
2tbsp olive oil, plus extra for greasing
400g (14oz) can chopped plum tomatoes
2 garlic cloves, crushed
2–3 sprigs of oregano
125g (4oz) mozzarella cheese, diced
50g (2oz) anchovy fillets, drained and
  halved lengthways
50g (2oz) pitted black olives

1 Tip the flour, yeast and ½ level tsp salt in a large bowl, stir then make a well in the centre. Pour 150ml (¼pint) warm water into the well and use a knife to mix everything together to make a dough.

2 Knead the dough on a floured surface for 5min or until smooth – it should be quite soft. Put the dough in a large, lightly oiled bowl, turn it to coat in the oil then cover the bowl with clingfilm and a clean tea towel. Place in a warm, draught-free place for 45min or until doubled in size.

3 Preheat the oven to 240°C (220°C in a fan oven), mark 9 and put a large baking sheet in the oven. Meanwhile, drain the canned tomatoes, mix with the garlic and season with freshly ground black pepper.

4 On a lightly floured surface, roll the dough into a 33x35.5cm (13x14in) rectangle and transfer to a large lightly oiled heavy-based baking sheet. Spread the tomato mixture over the dough, sprinkle with oregano and top with the mozzarella, anchovies and olives. Drizzle the 2tbsp oil over the pizza and season well.

5 Put the baking sheet on the hot baking sheet, and cook for 20–25min or until the cheese is golden and bubbling and the dough is lightly browned underneath. Cool on a wire rack for 5min before serving.

POPPY

The poppy is thought to have originated in the Mediterranean region, but is now widespread across the world, both as a cultivated plant and a wildflower. The plant has long been associated with cornfields – hence the common name of field poppy (*P. rhoeas*). The Romans regarded it as the sacred plant of Ceres, the goddess of corn. It was this species that bloomed so prolifically across the fields of Flanders during the terrible battles of the First World War and consequently became adopted as the symbol of remembrance. The opium poppy (*P. somniferum*) produces the essential ingredient of the painkilling drugs morphine and codeine, as well as the highly addictive morphine derivative heroin. Its cultivation is now carefully controlled. The herb has been used since ancient times. Poppy garlands have been found in Egyptian tombs and the sedative properties of the plant were utilised by the Egyptians. In Europe it was used as a treatment for dysentery and cholera. It was not an abused herb until the opium smoking habit hit China in the seventeenth century.

There are many different species of poppy; annual, biennial and perennial species offer a choice of colour and petal forms. The field poppy is a hardy annual that can grow 1.2m (4ft) high. It is almost too easy to grow and can swamp flower beds if allowed to self-seed. It has pale grey-green leaves on a slender stem, which is topped by the familiar bright red flower and succeeded by a bulbous grey-green seed head. At the base of each poppy petal there is usually a dramatic inky-purple or blue-black splash.

Collect the ripe seed for culinary use; if the seed is not fully ripe when collected it will deteriorate rapidly in store. To dry the seed heads for decorative use, hang them upside down in small bunches in an airy room. Place paper bags over the heads to stop them getting dusty and to avoid a liberal sprinkling of seeds on the floor.

Cultivation

The poppy likes well-drained soil in full sun. It is easy to grow from seed and will self-seed freely. Sow seed in spring or autumn where it is to flower and thin seedlings to 30cm (12in) apart.

Culinary use

The ripe seeds, which have a sweet, nutty flavour, are the only edible part of the plant. They can be sprinkled over the top of bread immediately prior to baking or crushed to thicken and flavour curries. The seeds of *P. rhoeas* and *P. somniferum* are alkaloid free and so safe for all culinary purposes, but I prefer to buy a bag of seeds for culinary use and keep the home-grown seeds for propagation.

Medicinal use

All parts of poppies are toxic save for the ripe seeds of *P. rhoeas* and *P. somniferum*, which are used in cooking.

Home and Beauty

Dried seed heads can be used in flower arrangements or to make table decorations or festive wreaths. They are beautiful unadorned, but children love to dip them in glitter or paint them for a more robust decorative style.

POPPY SEED GRANARY ROUND

Makes 8 rolls

15g (½oz) fresh yeast or 7g (¼oz) sachet
    dried yeast and ½tsp sugar
450g (1lb) granary bread flour
50g (2oz) butter
50g (2oz) Cheddar cheese, grated
25g (1oz) poppy seeds

1 Grease a 20.5cm (8in) sandwich tin. Put 300ml (½pint) warm water in a bowl and crumble in the fresh yeast. Stir until dissolved. (If using dried yeast, sprinkle it into water mixed with the sugar. Leave in a warm place for 15min until frothy.)
2 To make the dough, put the flour and 1 level tsp salt in a large bowl and rub in the butter. Add the cheese and the poppy seeds, reserving 1tsp to garnish. Stir in the yeast liquid and mix to a stiff dough.
3 Turn on to a lightly floured surface and knead for 10min until smooth. Put in a bowl, cover the bowl with clingfilm and leave to rise in a warm place for about 1hr until doubled in size.
4 Turn on to a lightly floured surface and knead for 2–3min until smooth.
5 Using a sharp knife, divide the dough into eight equal pieces and shape into neat, even-sized rolls with your hands.
6 Arrange the 'rolls' in the tin – seven around the edge and one in the middle. Cover with a clean cloth and leave to prove in a warm place for about 30min until doubled in size. Preheat the oven to 200ºC (180º in a fan oven), mark 6.
7 Sprinkle with the reserved poppy seeds. Bake for about 25min until golden brown and the bread sounds hollow when the bottom is tapped.

SCENTED-LEAVED GERANIUM

Today scented-leaved geraniums are more likely to be found in a display of summer bedding or in patio containers rather than in the herb garden. However, their aromatic leaves, which can yield a range of fragrances and flavours from rose to lemon, nutmeg and mint, justify their classification as herbs. The common name makes it easy to confuse these plants with cranesbill, which carries the genus name *Geranium*, but they are in fact entirely different plants. Scented-leaved geraniums are indigenous to South Africa and were brought to Europe in the seventeenth century. The French perfume industry quickly utilised their essential oil for commercial use.

A half-hardy evergreen that can grow 60cm (2ft) high, scented-leaved geraniums have pretty, aromatic lobed leaves. They carry small, pale pink, white or purple flowers throughout the summer.

Pick leaves throughout the growing season for use fresh or for drying. Harvest flowers when newly open.

Cultivation

Scented-leaved geraniums enjoy a sunny spot in well-drained soil. They can be grown from seed, but are so easy to propagate from stem cuttings that it is worth buying a few plants or begging some from friends. Take cuttings in spring or late summer, put into pots and keep very lightly watered throughout winter; if in doubt about watering fall on the side of healthy neglect. Scented-leaved geraniums make excellent container plants; they are tough and can withstand scant care and attention. However, the plants are not fully hardy so containers should be brought into a frost-free environment and garden plants lifted and potted up for the winter. Pots will rest happily on windowsills throughout the year.

Culinary use

The principal culinary geraniums include *Pelargonium graveolens*, which has a mint-rose scent and flavour, while *P.* 'Lemon Fancy' and *P.* 'Attar of Roses', as the names suggest, are respectively imbued with hints of lemon and rose. The species *P. crispum* should not be used for culinary purposes as it can cause stomach upsets so take great care to know your plants if you are using them for culinary purposes. Leaf flavours vary according to the variety, but all offer a gentle flavour and perfume that is delicious in ice creams, sorbets and summer drinks. The flowers can be crystallised and used to decorate cakes. The Victorians used to line cake tins with the leaves when baking plain sponges to impregnate them with a hint of the aroma. Grease and line the tin as usual, then place 20 leaves in the bottom of the tin before pouring over the sponge mixture. When the cake is cooked, allow it to cool before removing the paper and the leaves.

Medicinal use

The essential oil from the geranium is used in aromatherapy to relieve pre-menstrual tension and fluid retention. Geranium oil also often appears in herbal remedies designed to combat head lice in conjunction with the combing system.

Home and beauty

The fragrant leaves can be used in potpourri. Dry them whole and then crush or break them into the potpourri mix to release the smell. The essential oil added to bath water smells fabulous and will make a relaxing bath.

PARSLEY

Parsley has much to offer in the kitchen, but it also has many therapeutic properties. The ancient Greeks associated it with Archemorus, the herald of death, and planted it around tombs and used it to adorn the dead. The Romans took an entirely different view, using it extensively for culinary purposes and wearing it as protection against intoxication.

Parsley is rich in vitamins and minerals, containing iron, iodine, magnesium and masses of vitamin C. It is a natural diuretic and can be helpful in the treatment of hepatitis and rheumatic complaints. It is discreetly defined as a woman's herb, reputedly easing problems associated with menstrual flow and the menopause.

This frost-hardy biennial herb grows 30–50cm (12–20in) high and has bright green leaves. The most familiar parsley varieties are curly-leaved (*Petroselinum crispum*) and flat-leaf or French (*P. crispum* var. *neapolitanum*). Parsley is a cut-and-come-again plant, but take only a few sprigs at a time until it is established. Parsley will grow happily in the wild, given the right conditions, but it should never be gathered from the wild as it could be confused with the poisonous *Aethusa cynapium*, which it resembles.

Cut leaves for drying and freezing from early summer onwards.

Cultivation

Although parsley is a biennial, it is best grown as an annual. It likes warmth and is best sown in late spring or early summer in well-drained, fertile soil in a sunny or partly shaded position. It is easy to grow, but the seeds are slow to germinate. It does not like having its roots disturbed so sow in pots or plugs rather than seed trays. If sowing in spring, try soaking the seeds overnight in warm water or after sowing pour on boiling water to speed up germination. The later you sow the faster the seeds will germinate; however, as plants have to be established before harvesting, an early sowing makes good sense. If sowing directly into the ground it can be helpful to sow some lettuce or radish in the drill; these germinate faster than the parsley and act as a marker for your potential parsley crop. With such a clear visual reference you can also weed without fear of accidentally pulling up the parsley. Six or seven plants should produce a steady supply of leaves. A second crop can be sown later in summer and if a fresh year-round supply is called for grow in pots, in a greenhouse or on a kitchen windowsill.

Culinary use

Flat-leaf, or French, parsley is recommended for use in the kitchen for its superior flavour and texture. It is used heavily in Middle Eastern cookery, notably with basil and mint. In general it combines well with other herbs and forms part of the classic herb mixes of *bouquet garni* (*see page 172*) and *fines herbes*. The latter is recommended for dishes featuring eggs and is a classic for flavouring omelettes.

Medicinal use

Hot parsley tea is a tonic and diuretic and is thought to remove excess fluid from the body. It is useful in treating kidney, bladder and urinary tract infections. During the Second World War soldiers in the trenches drunk it in the hope of combating dysentery-induced kidney problems. To make the tea simply pour hot water over a few sprigs of parsley and leave for a few minutes to infuse; strain before drinking.

Parsley tea is also said to increase the production of breast milk. But as it also both stimulates and soothes uterine muscles, it is not recommended for use during pregnancy. Parsley is a well-known breath freshener; try chewing some leaves after a meal laced with garlic. It can also be used in poultices to make antiseptic dressings for wounds and insect bites.

Home and beauty

Families suffering from infestations of head lice may want to try the parsley tea cure, which is said to kill the lice. Make the tea by pouring boiling water over crushed dried seeds, not leaves, and leave for a few minutes to infuse before straining the liquid. Wash and rinse the hair as usual, then pour the tea over the hair and wrap the scalp in towels for 30 minutes. Then remove the towels and allow the hair to dry naturally without rinsing it. I have yet to test this out myself (lice never visit when you want them), but I would also comb with a fine-toothed lice comb as part of the elimination process.

LUXURY SALMON AND PARSLEY FISHCAKES

Makes 16

350g (12oz) poached fresh salmon, flaked
225g (8oz) smoked salmon, roughly chopped
350g (12oz) freshly cooked mashed potato
1tbsp lemon juice
75g (3oz) butter, melted
2tbsp freshly chopped parsley
2 medium eggs, beaten
About 225g (8oz) dried white breadcrumbs
Vegetable oil, for frying

1 Mix the fresh and smoked salmon with the mashed potato, lemon juice, butter and parsley and season with freshly ground black pepper. Add just enough beaten egg to bind the mixture together. It should be firm, not sloppy. Cool, if necessary, then chill for 1hr or until very firm.

2 Shape the mixture into 16 cakes about 2.5cm (1in) thick. Brush each fishcake with some of the remaining beaten egg and coat with breadcrumbs. Chill for 30min to firm up.

3 Coat the fishcakes with egg and breadcrumbs once more. Chill again until firm. Preheat the oven to 130ºC (110ºC in a fan oven), mark ½.

4 Heat some oil in a large frying pan and shallow-fry the fishcakes in batches for 3–4min on each side, or until golden brown. Drain on absorbent kitchen paper and keep warm in the oven until all the fishcakes are cooked.

COWSLIP

The cowslip is indigenous to Europe and temperate Asia, where it grows wild in pastures, meadows, fields and woods. It was once an important herb, being regarded as a general panacea for all manner of complaints. Its common name is derived from the old English word *cuslyppe* for a cowpat, and is a reference to the plant's habit of springing up wherever a cow had left its mark. Modern farming practices have made this once common plant a rarity in the wild, but fortunately it will grow happily in the garden, given suitable conditions. The plant's flowers were thought to resemble a bunch of keys and so it was dedicated to the Apostle Peter, the gatekeeper to heaven, hence its other common name, herb Peter.

A low-growing perennial, the cowslip grows 30cm (12in) high. It has textural oval leaves in a basal rosette from which rise long stems, which bear clusters of yellow flowers from mid- to late spring. These are attractive to butterflies and bees.

Pick leaves and flowers to use fresh as required.

Cultivation

Cowslips enjoy moist, but well-drained, lime-rich soil in semi-shade. Seed is best sown fresh in early autumn, so for best results use a specialist seed supplier. Sow into a seed tray, cover with glass and place outdoors or in a cool place. The seed will germinate in six to eight weeks. Plant out in spring when the plants are large enough to handle. If naturalising cowslips in grass mow around them until after they have set seed. Cowslip is easy to propagate by division.

Culinary use

Cowslip leaves can be eaten fresh or cooked, although they are not to everyone's taste. The flowers can be mixed into salads or used as cake decorations. Cowslip wine is an interesting and palatable drink for home-brewing enthusiasts to try making, if enough flowers are available.

Medicinal use

Cowslip has antispasmodic and sedative properties. The roots can be used for the treatment of whooping cough and bronchial complaints as well as arthritis. Cowslip tea is reputed to ease insomnia, headaches and constipation and may help to calm hyperactive or insomniac children. Compresses applied to the head can bring some relief from migraine. The essential oil works similarly to arnica and can reduce swelling and bruising. Some people react to primrose adversely; they can experience a form of contact dermatitis (primula dermatitis) after handling the plant and its products.

PRIMROSE

The primrose is an enchanting little wildflower with a retiring disposition. A native European, it is seen growing in the wild all too infrequently as its natural hedgerow habitat has been severely eroded by intensive farming practices. However, a new awareness amongst farmers, and laws that make it illegal to gather or dig up wildflowers, are having a positive impact. The plant has many herbal properties and merits being found a shady corner in any garden. Moreover, the more it is cultivated, the greater its chances of re-establishing itself in the wild.

The flowers are favoured by bees, but often appear too early for many insects to pollinate them, as observed by Shakespeare in *The Winter's Tale* with his reference to 'pale primroses that die unmarried'. Queen Victoria was fond of them, too. She sent a box of primroses from her favourite residence, Osborne House on the Isle of Wight, to her long-serving prime minister, Benjamin Disraeli, when he was dying. The flowers have been associated with him ever since and the Primrose League was the name of the group that continued to promote his principles of government long after his death.

The herb is an astringent, an antispasmodic and an emetic. It was widely used during the Middle Ages as a treatment for gout and rheumatism, but its medicinal use waned when other herbs came to be regarded as more effective.

The primrose is a low-growing perennial with rosettes of deeply veined oval leaves. The perfect little yellow flowers appear from mid- to late spring.

Pick flowers to use fresh or to crystallise for cake decoration.

Cultivation

Primroses enjoy dappled shade and a moist soil. Sow seed in autumn or early winter in a seed tray. Cover with glass and place outside – the seeds need exposure to the cold to germinate – and be prepared to wait for up to two years. When the seedlings are large enough to handle, plant out at 15cm (6in) intervals. Fortunately, primrose plants are very easy to lift and divide; garden centres can supply plants to get you started.

Culinary use

The primrose does not have many culinary uses, but the flowers are a delicious addition to green salads. They taste like an insipid, perfumed berry and can be crystallised to make exquisite cake decorations (*see opposite and page 44*). Crystallised flowers are easy to make and enable you to produce impressively decorated cakes with very little effort.

Medicinal use

The primrose has sedative and expectorant properties. Leaves, flowers and roots can all be used to make an infusion designed to relieve coughs and act as a mild sedative.

CRYSTALLISED
PRIMROSES

1 egg white
White caster sugar
Freshly picked primrose flowers

1 Preheat the oven to 140°C (120°C in a
fan oven), mark 1. Add a pinch of salt to
the egg white and beat lightly, without
allowing it to become frothy.
2 Cover a baking sheet with greaseproof
paper and sprinkle with caster sugar. Dip
each primrose flower in the beaten egg
white, then place on the baking sheet and
sprinkle lightly with more sugar.
3 Cover the flowers with another sheet
of greaseproof paper and put them in
the oven with the door ajar for 3–4hr.
Alternatively, place the flowers in an
airing cupboard until dry.

Store the crystallised flowers in an airtight container and use within two days.

BLACKTHORN, SLOE

sloe gin

Makes 900ml (1½pints)

450g (1lb) sloes, stalked and
   cleaned

75–125g (3–4oz) golden
   granulated sugar

Few drops of almond essence

900ml (1½pints) gin

1 Prick the sloes all over with a clean skewer and put into a large screw-top jar. Add the sugar and a few drops of almond essence. Fill up the jar with gin, screw the lid on tightly and leave in a cool dark place for 3 months, shaking occasionally.

2 At the end of this time, open the jar and strain through muslin until clear. Rebottle, cork and leave until required.

➔ If made in mid-autumn, the drink will be ready for Christmas, but it will improve with age if you want to keep it longer.

The blackthorn is an inconspicuous, thorny shrub or small tree, which bears a delicious, damson-like fruit – the sloe. The fruit, which has a uniquely strong and astringent flavour, gives blackthorn its herbal classification. Enthusiasts of sloe gin are always on the look-out for this plant and claim it is hard to find. In fact it is indigenous to Europe, North Africa and western Asia and is much in evidence in the countryside, where it is a useful hedging plant. Its sharp thorns make it an effective barrier with the added benefit of a home-grown crop of sloes. It blends well with other native species, such as hawthorn or May, wild rose and holly for a traditional hedgerow mix. The wood, which is very hard, is excellent for making walking sticks. In Ireland it is traditionally used for fashioning the stout cudgels known as *shillelaghs*.

Sloes can be gathered from the wild with impunity, but the key to finding a good supply in the autumn is to identify the plants in spring when they are in bloom. Blackthorn flowers in the bitterest, coldest days of early spring, when its bare branches are smothered in fine white blossom. Make a mental note of the location of the blackthorn bushes in your area and return in the autumn. The deep blue fruit is ready for picking in mid- to late autumn. Always wear protective gloves to go sloe picking as the thorns are wickedly sharp.

Cultivation

The blackthorn is quite tolerant of aspect, but dislikes soil that is too wet or too dry. Plant in early autumn while the soil is still warm. Space plants at 60cm (2ft) intervals for hedging.

Culinary use

The sour fruits are one of the two essential ingredients of sloe gin, the other being the spirit itself. This is a delicious, warming drink with a distinctive flavour of a fruit spirit combined with the sharp dryness of the gin. Sloe jelly has a wonderfully sharp flavour and is a good accompaniment to rich meat such as pork and game.

SLOE AND APPLE JELLY

Makes 1.8kg (4lb)

900g (2lb) sloes
Grated rind and juice of 1 lemon
1.8kg (4lb) apples, roughly chopped
        without peeling or coring
About 900g (2lb) preserving or golden
        granulated sugar (see method)

1 Prick the sloes with a fork. Put them in a large pan with the lemon rind and juice and 1tbsp water. Simmer until the fruit has cooked to a pulp and the juices are running freely, about 20–30min.

2 Meanwhile, cook the apples with a little water in another pan for about 15min, until pulpy. Strain the contents of both pans through several layers of muslin. Reserve the juice; discard the fruit pulp.

3 Preheat the oven to 140°C (120°C in a fan oven), mark 1. Measure the combined juice from the two fruit. Measure out 450g (1lb) sugar for every 600ml (1pint) liquid. Place the sugar in a heatproof bowl and warm in the oven for 2–3min. To sterilise some jam jars, wash them in very hot soapy water, rinse them well then place them in the warm oven to dry.

4 Return the fruit juices to a clean pan and set over a medium heat. Stir in the warmed sugar until dissolved. Boil for 10min until it has reached setting point. Test for this by spooning some jelly on to a chilled saucer; if it wrinkles when you push it with a finger, it has reached setting point. If it does not wrinkle, boil for a few minutes more and try again. Remove any scum with a slotted spoon.

5 Let the jelly cool slightly then pour into the warmed sterilised jars. Cover immediately with waxed discs. Leave to go cold then cover the jars with cellophane held with an elastic band. Label, store in a cool place and use within six months.

ROSE

Some roses have cosmetic, gastronomic and medicinal uses and have been cultivated in herb gardens for centuries. The apothecary's rose (*R. gallica*), a deciduous shrub with pinkish-red roses and native to southern and central Europe, is said to be the oldest form of rose in cultivation. Its strongly scented double flowers bloom from late spring to early summer. These roses were found in Tutankhamun's tomb, purportedly left by his wife as a symbol of their love. The Romans also associated the rose with love, and decorated statues of Venus and Cupid with the flowers. They also used rose petals for strewing.

The dog rose (*R. canina*), also a deciduous shrub, is indigenous to Europe and North Africa. It is found growing wild in hedgerows and produces delicate five-petalled flowers, which are followed by bright red hips. We know that these were a food source thousands of years ago as the seeds have been found among the remains of a Neolithic woman unearthed in Britain. During the Middle Ages the hips were served as desserts, but it was not until the 1930s that rose hips were discovered to contain more vitamin C than any other fruit or vegetable – 20 times more than in the equivalent weight of oranges. When fruit and vegetable shortages began in the Second World War a national campaign urged volunteers to collected hundreds of tons of hips to be processed into rose-hip syrup in an effort to keep the nation healthy. Some children prefer to make itching powder from hips – the hairs lining the hips and attached to the seeds are irritants.

Pick the petals of the apothecary's rose on a dry day before the petals are fully open, remove the stamens and dry quickly. Store the petals in a dry place and use within four months, after which time all their medicinal properties will be lost. Gather hips from the dog rose when ripe after the first frost. Cut them lengthways and dry rapidly. Shake the dried hips in a wire sieve to remove the hairs and store in a cool place. Use dried hips within a year, before their nutritional value is lost.

Cultivation

Roses enjoy humus-rich, well-drained soil in sun or semi-shade. Old roses (as opposed to modern cultivars) can be bought from specialist nurseries while the dog rose is very easy to propagate from hips. Gather some hips and let them mature in the open air before sowing in a pot in late autumn. Deadhead flowers in the summer to promote flowering and prune in spring to keep bushes open and airy.

Culinary use

Roses can be used to make rosewater and rose syrups for flavouring desserts and ices. The Turks are the flowers' greatest devotees and use rosewater to flavour Turkish delight. Rose flavouring is also used extensively in Tunisia, Morocco and Algeria. Rose petals can be used in fruit drinks, wine, jellies and jams. They can also be candied or crystallised for decorating cakes. Both petals and hips can be used to make tea.

Medicinal use

Rose hips are an excellent source of vitamins C, B and E. The essential oil from the petals, which is used in aromatherapy, is believed to aid circulation and cleanse the blood. An infusion of rose petals is claimed to restore the balance of gut flora after a course of antibiotics. It can also be used as a soothing compress for eye infections. Simply infuse a small handful of petals in 1 litre (1¾pints) freshly boiled water for five to ten minutes.

Home and beauty

Rose petals and buds can be dried for potpourri. Rosewater is a gentle tonic for mature and sensitive skins.

ROSE-HIP
SYRUP

Makes 600ml (1pint)
900g (2lb) ripe rose hips
450g (1lb) granulated sugar

1 Put small clean bottles to warm in a
very low oven before you begin. Wash the
rose hips, remove the stalks and calyces
and chop coarsely in a food processor.
2 Bring 2.3litres (4pints) water to the boil
in a pan and add the chopped hips.
Return to the boil, remove from the heat
and leave to stand for 15min. Strain
through a piece of muslin, squeezing the
pulp to extract as much juice as possible.
This straining process is important, as the
prickly seeds can be an internal irritant.
Reserve the strained liquid.
3 Return the pulp to the pan and pour in
1litre (1¾pints) water. Bring to the boil
then remove from the heat and leave to
stand for 10min before repeating the
straining process.
4 Transfer both amounts of strained liquid
to a pan and boil until reduced to around
1litre (1¾pints) of liquid. Stir in the sugar
until dissolved, return to the boil and continue to boil for 5min. Pour the syrup into
the warmed bottles and seal.

This is my mother's recipe, which I used
to enjoy as a child. It is packed with vitamin C. It is delicious but very sweet – if
you prefer a sharper flavour, halve the
amount of sugar. Use small bottles whenever possible because the syrup does not
keep for long once a bottle has been
opened. I cannot vouch for how long the
syrup lasts in sealed bottles. My family
was inclined to turn a blind eye to a
little mould or fermentation, which is no
recommendation.

ROSEMARY

see page 27

rosemary water

4tbsp fresh rosemary flowering tips
150ml (¼pint) ethyl alcohol

1 Put both ingredients in an airtight jar and leave in a cool dark place for two weeks. Shake occasionally during this time.
2 Strain the liquid into a clean, dry bottle and seal.
➔ Use rosemary water externally to soothe aches, as you would witchhazel.

At once pretty and useful, aromatic rosemary is a herb garden essential that has many uses in the kitchen and the home. It is indigenous to the Mediterranean region and steeped in history and tradition. Its name is derived from the Latin *ros-marinus*, which means 'dew of the sea' and alludes to its favoured seaside habitat. Traditionally, rosemary was a symbol of love, friendship and fidelity, which is why brides once wore wreaths made with the herb. It was also reputed to strengthen the brain and the memory so ancient Greek and Roman scholars used to twine it in their hair in the belief it would help them to learn. Shakespeare alluded to its supposed power in *Hamlet* with the famous line: 'There's rosemary, that's for remembrance.'

An evergreen shrub, rosemary has small spiky leaves, green on top and silvery underneath, and produces tiny whorls of mauve, blue or white flowers throughout summer. It grows slowly, but can reach an impressive 2m (just over 6ft) or more in time. Rosemary can make a decorative hedge in a sunny situation (*see page 27*); prostrate varieties are also available. Grow rosemary where you can brush your hands against it as you pass and breathe in the wonderfully invigorating fragrance that is released.

Rosemary is an easy herb to dry, but as the plant is evergreen it is best to simply pick leaves as required. However, if you do need to dry rosemary do so in the autumn when the plant produces fresh new shoots.

Cultivation

Rosemary is happiest in a sunny, sheltered spot, ideally on a south- or south-west-facing wall. As it can be damaged by frost, try not to trim or prune it until all danger of frost has passed. If you are subject to harsh winters grow rosemary in a pot and move it to a protected position during winter. Rosemary can be grown from seed, but as cuttings are so easy this is the favoured method of propagation. Take cuttings in late summer and plant out the following spring. Layering is another effective method of increasing stock. Prune the plant in summer after flowering to keep it in good shape. Rosemary plants are more productive if replaced every five or six years.

Culinary use

Rosemary is a popular culinary herb much used in France and Italy and is one of the ingredients of the *herbes de Provence* mix. However, its flavour has a hint of camphor that does not blend readily with other herbs so it is usually best used alone. It is much used with meat, notably lamb and fish. A simple sprig thrown in with a joint or some pan-fried steaks greatly enhances the flavour of the meat. The herb will transform a barbecue. Add a sprig to a bottle of wine vinegar or oil to make a wonderful culinary flavouring or mix a couple of tablespoons of freshly chopped rosemary leaves into bread dough for delicious herb bread.

Medicinal use

Rosemary is reputed to be good for the digestion and to help stimulate circulation, while the essential oil has antibacterial and antifungicidal properties. Rosemary tea, a delicious, reviving drink, has the bonus of being a good mouthwash for anyone suffering from bad breath. Drinking small amounts of the tea is reputed to ease flatulence. To make the tea simply pour boiling water over one teaspoon of freshly chopped leaves, or just use a sprig of the herb. Leave to infuse for five minutes before straining out the herb. You can add honey if you wish to sweeten it.

Home and beauty

Like lavender, the dried herb can be used to fill muslin bags for placing in drawers and wardrobes, where it will help keep clothes smelling sweet and discourage moths. If you make your own candles, adding some torn rosemary and sage leaves to the liquid candle wax will repel insects when the candles are lit. Rosemary water can be used to soothe aches, like witchhazel. A rosemary hair rinse will strengthen and deepen the colour of dark and red hair. If you tie a few rosemary sprigs under the hot tap when running the water, you will be rewarded with a refreshing and invigorating bath.

GARLIC AND ROSEMARY SCENTED LEG OF LAMB

Serves 8

2.7kg (6lb) leg of lamb
3 garlic cloves, peeled and cut into slivers
Small bunch of sprigs of rosemary
2tbsp olive oil
150ml (¼pint) red wine
300ml (½pint) hot lamb stock

1 Preheat the oven to 230°C (210°C in a fan oven), mark 8. Weigh the lamb and calculate the cooking time, allowing 15–20min per 450g (11b), depending on how well done you like lamb. Make small incisions in the skin of the lamb all over and insert a tiny sprig of rosemary and a sliver of garlic into each slit.

2 Rub the lamb with the olive oil and season with plenty of freshly ground black pepper. Put in a roasting tin and roast for 15min. Reduce the temperature to 200°C (180°C in a fan oven), mark 6 and continue to cook for 1¼–1¾hr, basting occasionally.

3 Put the lamb on a board or warm serving plate, cover with foil and leave to rest for 15min. Drain off the fat from the roasting tin and discard. Put the tin on the hob, add the red wine and stock and bring to the boil, stirring to deglaze and dissolve any of the goodness on the bottom. Boil to reduce, then season to taste with salt and freshly ground black pepper. Strain, if necessary, into a warm jug and serve with the roast lamb.

BLACKBERRY

blackberry decoction

25g (1oz) dried blackberry leaves

1 Put 900ml (1½pints) water in a pan and bring to the boil. Add the blackberry leaves and continue to boil for 5min. Remove from the heat and leave to infuse for 10min.

2 Strain the liquid and discard the leaves before drinking.

➔ Drink 1 cup up to three times a day to treat diarrhoea, piles or cystitis, or use as a gargle for sore throats and mouth ulcers.

The delight of coming unexpectedly on a blackberry bush heavy with fruit is hard to define – perhaps blackberrying appeals to our basic hunter-gatherer instinct. Fortunately the blackberry, which is indigenous to Europe, is abundant and prolific and the fruit can be gathered with impunity. The plant has been used since prehistoric times and the seeds of the fruit have been discovered among the remains of a Neolithic man in Britain. The blackberry is a feature of British country churchyards as it used to be planted to keep grazing sheep away from the graves. The berries have obvious appeal, but in addition the plant has medicinal properties, which have long been valued: the ancient Greeks used it for treating gout, whilst the Romans used it to relieve inflammation of the bowel. It also has astringent properties and is high in vitamin C and tannin.

The blackberry is an untidy deciduous shrub that can grow 3m (10ft) high. Its thorny biennial stems bear lobed toothed leaves. The pink and white flowers, which appear in clusters on mature shoots in summer, are followed by the blackberries from late summer to early autumn.

The berries bruise easily so treat them with care when harvesting. Handle and wash them as little as is possible.

Cultivation

Blackberry bushes will grow just about anywhere and can easily become a problem if not contained. They enjoy moist but well-drained soil in a sunny spot. Propagate by layering in summer; rooting should occur by mid-autumn, when the young plant can be severed from its parent. Autumn is the best time for planting blackberry canes. They are best grown trained against a fence or wall. Cut the plants back to 30cm (12in) above the ground each autumn to encourage healthy new growth and help eliminate disease.

Culinary use

The large juicy berries are not often served as a fruit alone, as they lack a little texture and sharpness. However, they are sublime teamed with cooking apples in a pie or crumble and produce a deep red fruit compote or summer pudding. They can also be used to make syrups and wine. Bramble jelly is the most delicious conserve I have ever tasted and is very easy to make. Blackberry leaves mixed with raspberry leaves make a delicious tea.

Medicinal use

A decoction of blackberry leaves is reputed to be an effective treatment for diarrhoea, piles and cystitis; you can drink up to three cups a day. It can also be used as a gargle to ease sore throats and mouth ulcers.

APPLE AND BLACKBERRY PIE

Serves 6

For the pastry

175g (6oz) plain flour, sifted, plus extra
    for dusting

75g (3oz) butter, diced and chilled

1 level tbsp golden caster sugar

1 medium egg yolk

For the filling

225g (8oz) blackberries, washed
    and drained

700g (1½lb) cooking apples, peeled,
    cored and thickly sliced

125g (4oz) golden caster sugar, plus
    extra for sprinkling

A little milk, for glazing

1 Preheat the oven to 220°C (200°C in a fan oven), mark 7.

2 Put the flour in a food processor. Add the butter and whiz until the mixture resembles fine breadcrumbs. Tip into a bowl, stir in the sugar. Mix the egg yolk with 1tbsp cold water then stir into the flour mixture. Knead lightly to bring the mixture together. Place the ball of dough in a polythene bag and chill.

3 Meanwhile, put the blackberries in a pan. Add water to cover and cook for 5min over a medium heat until tender.

4 Put the apples, sugar and blackberries in a 900ml (1½ pint) pie dish. Roll out the pastry on a lightly floured work surface to a size to cover the pie dish. Lift into place, trimming off the excess pastry around the edges of the dish.

5 Brush the pie with milk then sprinkle with sugar. Slash the top with a knife then bake for 10min. Reduce the oven temperature to 180°C (160°C in a fan oven), mark 4 and continue to cook for 20–30min. Serve with vanilla ice cream.

SORREL

There are two varieties of sorrel, which occur naturally in grasslands of Europe and Asia. One is more favoured as a culinary herb, the other as a medicinal herb. The ancient Egyptians and the Romans used sorrel to settle the stomach after overeating. Roman soldiers used to suck the leaves to take the edge off their thirst. This habit gave the plant its genus name *Rumex*, which comes from the Latin *rumo*, meaning 'I suck'. During the Middle Ages sorrel was a popular salad leaf and potherb. The herb has diuretic and cooling properties and, like spinach, it is high in vitamins A, B and C and rich in potassium.

French, or buckler leaf, sorrel (*R. scutatus*) is more favoured for culinary use. The leaves have a sharp flavour with a lemony zest. They are smaller than those of common sorrel and the flavour is less bitter. Common or garden sorrel (*R. acetosa*) has a very strong flavour. The juice from the leaves and stems of this variety can curdle milk and as it reacts badly with iron leaves should be cooked in a stainless steel pan only. Both of these perennial plants can be identified by the shape of their leaves: those of French sorrel are shaped like a shield while those of common sorrel are lance shaped. Both plants grow 15–30cm (6–12in) high, carry flowers in early to mid-summer and acquire a reddish hue as the season progresses.

Pick sorrel as required to use fresh or to freeze.

Cultivation

French sorrel enjoys a rich and acid, moisture-retentive soil in sun or partial shade. Sow the seeds in late spring in a prepared site and thin the seedlings to 10cm (4in) apart. The plant runs to seed quickly so remove flower heads as soon as they appear. As the young leaves have the sweetest flavour it is advisable to make successive sowings to ensure a continuous supply through the summer. Common sorrel grows wild.

Culinary use

The use of sorrel as a culinary herb fell out of favour in Britain after the Middle Ages. The French, however, have always recognised its potential. They use it raw in salads and cook it in soups and sauces. The tart but sweet and juicy flavour of French sorrel brings a zing to mild dishes, notably omelettes. Sprinkle freshly chopped leaves with a light hand. Buckler-leaf sorrel has a wonderful lemony taste and my daughter – who abhors all greens – eats it with relish.

Medicinal use

Common sorrel is high in oxalic acid and should not be used frequently as it can lead to the formation of tiny stones of calcium oxalate. Anyone suffering from bladder stones, gout, rheumatism and pulmonary complaints should avoid it altogether. However, it is reputed to be helpful in treating diarrhoea, stomach upsets and urinary infections.

Home and beauty

The acidic sap of sorrel can be used to bleach out unsightly rust and ink stains from white linen.

SORREL SOUFFLÉ

Serves 4

125g (4oz) sorrel
50g (2oz) butter
225g (8oz) button mushrooms,
    finely chopped
1 garlic clove, crushed
3 level tbsp plain flour
200ml (7fl oz) milk
225g (8oz) Fontina or Gruyère cheese,
    rinded and grated
3 medium eggs, separated

1 Preheat the oven to 190°C (170°C in a fan oven), mark 5. Trim any tough stalks off the sorrel. Wash and drain the leaves then finely chop.

2 Melt the butter in a large pan, add the sorrel, mushrooms and crushed garlic. Stir over a high heat for 1–2 min. Stir in the flour and continue to cook for 1min.

3 Remove the pan from the heat and gradually stir in the milk to make a smooth sauce. Bring to the boil, stirring, then cook for 1min.

4 Remove from the heat and beat in 200g (7oz) of the cheese followed by the egg yolks. Season well with salt and freshly ground black pepper.

5 Whisk the egg whites until stiff but not dry. Fold lightly into the sauce mixture. Spoon into a 1.4litre (2½pint) greased soufflé dish and sprinkle over the remaining grated cheese to coat evenly.

6 Bake for about 40min or until well risen, browned and just set. Serve at once.

SAGE

The genus name *Salvia* is derived from the Latin *salvere*, which means 'to save' or 'to heal' and, as its name suggests, the plant is an important medicinal, as well as culinary, herb. As there are over 750 species of salvia, ranging from annuals to shrubs, it is important to choose carefully. *Salvia officinalis* is the most useful culinary herb and is the plant most commonly associated with the name.

The earliest records show that sage was popular with herbalists in China, Asia, Europe and Iceland. The ancient Greeks and the Romans used it as a tonic for both the mind and the body. It was widely believed to be good for the brain, the senses and the memory, and recent medical research has indicated that it may well be beneficial in helping to treat the degenerative brain disease known as Alzheimer's. Sage is also a useful culinary herb, reputed to aid digestion. It also contains powerful antioxidants, which slow spoilage, allowing it to work effectively as a natural preservative.

Salvia officinalis is a low-growing evergreen shrub, which grows approximately 30cm (12in) high. Its velvety soft leaves are a dull grey-green and the flowers, which bloom in summer, are blue or mauve. Although indigenous to the Mediterranean, it is sufficiently hardy to be able to tolerate fairly hard winters in more northern climates as long as the soil is well drained.

As an evergreen, sage offers a plentiful supply of fresh leaves all year round, but if you wish to dry the herb, harvest the leaves in early summer before the flowers appear. Unfortunately, sage is not the easiest herb to dry successfully and can go mouldy if it is not dried slowly or stored in an airtight jar.

Cultivation

Sage is happiest in a warm, sunny spot and is a good plant to grow in a gap between paving stones or in pots. *S. officinalis* can be grown from seed, but you will not be able to pick leaves until the plant is in its second year. For faster results try propagating from softwood cuttings taken in late spring or early summer. Layering in spring can also be successful if the plant is mature and straggly. Cut back woody stems in early spring to encourage bushy growth, but be prepared to replace plants every five years, as they become straggly.

Culinary use

In the kitchen sage is used to flavour meat, soups and fish. Due to its digestive properties it is most commonly associated with fatty meat like pork or duck. The flavour and smell are singular and hard to describe – somewhat warm, aromatic and bitter. As the flavour does not mix readily with other herbs, sage is best used on its own. It is a good choice for making a herb oil or vinegar and its antiseptic properties make it a useful culinary preservative.

Medicinal use

Sage is a natural antiseptic. It is believed to be a good tonic for the nerves and a stimulant for the circulation. The herb is especially useful for women as it can help to regulate periods and diminish the hot flushes associated with the menopause. Fresh sage tea has been recommended for convalescents and anyone under mental stress. It also aids digestion. Gargling with sage tea mixed with a little cider vinegar will soothe infected gums, mouth ulcers, sore throats and laryngitis. Sage and vinegar are traditionally combined for use in compresses and poultices, and are reputed to be effective for easing sprains and bruising – the vinegar brings the bruise to the surface and reduces swelling, while the sage soothes and heals.

SAGE AND ONION STUFFING

Makes enough stuffing for a 1.4kg
  (3lb) oven-ready chicken
1tbsp oil
75g (3oz) onion, peeled and chopped
125g (4oz) pork sausagemeat
1tbsp finely chopped fresh sage

1 Heat the oil in a pan, add the onion and
cook gently for 7–10min, until soft and
golden. Turn into a bowl and allow to cool.
2 Add the sausagemeat and sage to the
cooled onion mixture and season with salt
and freshly ground black pepper. Mix
everything together well and use to stuff
a chicken for roasting.

ELDER

The elder, or elderberry, is a common wild plant with innumerable herbal uses. It is
indigenous to Europe, western Asia and North Africa and grows wild in woodlands, at
roadsides and on waste ground. It was formerly a standard feature in most herb gardens
as its spirit was believed to protect all other herbs. There are many legends associated
with it and in the past elder leaves were attached to windows and doors on the last day
of April to deter witches. For the same reason elder was commonly planted near the
back door of a house. It was also believed that anyone standing under an elder tree at
midnight on Midsummer's Eve might catch a glimpse of the King of the Elves and his
retinue. According to one Christian tradition the cross on which Jesus was crucified was
made from the wood of an elder, and in another Judas was purported to have hanged
himself from an elder tree.

The elder is a large deciduous shrub or small tree that can grow 4.5m (just
under 15ft) high. It carries oval serrated leaves and flat heads of tiny creamy white flowers
in late spring and early summer. These are followed in early autumn by bunches of
berries, which are a purple-black when fully ripe.

Gather the flowers early in the season for the best flavour; if gathered late the
flavour and perfume can be overpoweringly sickly. Handle them very gently for they are
easily damaged. To dry the flowers place them face down on fine gauze. Harvest the ripe
berries to use fresh as required.

Cultivation

Elder tolerates most soils, but
enjoys a sunny position. Gather a few ripe
berries from the wild, put them in a pot of
compost and place out of doors. When the
seedlings are big enough to handle plant
them out in the garden. The plants will
flower within three years. The elder needs
to be kept in check or it will rapidly domi-
nate the garden. Prune very hard every
autumn. The plant self-seeds freely.

Culinary use

Elderflowers have a superbly
subtle flavour, commonly likened to that
of Muscat grapes. They can be used to
make delicious cordials, syrups, ices,
desserts and jams. The flowers can be
dipped in a light batter and fried to make
fritters. Elderberries are rich in vitamin C
and can be used to make the most
tasty jams and conserves. Elderflower
and elderberry wines are notorious home-
brewing favourites.

Medicinal use

Elderflowers are said to help
reduce levels of catarrh and were commonly used to relieve colds, coughs and
influenza. They can be helpful in relieving
some of the symptoms of hay fever, as
well as for treating sciatica, rheumatism
and cystitis. Flower infusions soothe sore
throats and, used as a compress, can
relieve conjunctivitis. Both flowers and
berries have a mild laxative action. An
elderberry conserve is said to ease
headaches and neuralgia.

Home and beauty

Elderflower water is claimed to
whiten and soften the skin and to help
eliminate freckles.

ELDERFLOWER CORDIAL

Makes about 2litres (3½pints)
10 large elderflower heads
900g (2lb) sugar
2 lemons, washed and sliced
25g (1oz) tartaric acid

1 Put all the ingredients in a bowl. Add 2.3litres (4pints) boiling water then cover and leave for 24hr, stirring occasionally.
2 Put small clean bottles to warm in a very low oven. Strain the elderflower mixture through layers of muslin, then pour the cordial into the sterilised bottles. Seal and leave for two to three weeks.
3 Dilute to taste with sparkling mineral water. Once opened, use within two to three days.

SALAD BURNET

Salad burnet is a tasty little herb that is widely grown in France. Its leaves are delicious in salads and is an easy plant to cultivate. It was much prized in centuries past for its ability to provide green leaves throughout the winter when other greens were scarce. The name is derived from the Latin *sanguis sorbere*, which means 'to absorb blood' and refers to the fact that the herb was traditionally used to staunch the flow of blood from wounds. Salad burnet was a favourite herb in Tudor herb and knot gardens and was transported to the New World by the Pilgrim Fathers.

A hardy perennial, salad burnet will produce attractive greenery right through mild winters. It will grow equally happily in sun or shade, but enjoys a chalky soil. The leaves form a flat rosette, each one made up of opposing pairs of toothed leaflets. The flowering stems grow 30cm (12in) high and carry small deep crimson flowers throughout summer.

To guarantee a good continuous harvest, keep cutting the flower heads back. Although the herb may well survive the winter it is sensible to sow a new crop every year, as the newer leaves are the most delicious.

Cultivation

Salad burnet grows only from seed, but once *in situ* it will self-seed freely in the right conditions. Sow seed in a seed tray in spring. Harden off and plant out at 30cm (12in) intervals. For culinary purposes the herb is best treated as an annual. In the garden, this plant makes an attractive path edging.

Culinary use

As its name suggests, salad burnet is especially useful for salads. The youngest leaves are the tastiest and have a delicious nutty, cucumber flavour. They are delicious chopped and added to soft cheese dips. They can be used in soups and stews and to replace parsley as a garnish. Salad burnet makes superb herb vinegar for use in salad dressings.

Medicinal use

The herb has diuretic and astringent properties. It increases rates of perspiration, aids digestion and has been used to treat gout and rheumatism. An infusion is said to relieve diarrhoea and haemorrhoids. You can use lightly crushed leaves as a compress to treat headaches.

Home and beauty

An infusion of salad burnet will refresh mature skins.

COTTON LAVENDER

Cotton lavender or santolina is a very pretty bushy herb with a strong aromatic fragrance. Indigenous to the Mediterranean region, the plant is actually a member of the daisy family and is not lavender at all. It was formerly much used medicinally, but has been replaced by more effective herbs. Cotton lavender is an effective insect repellent, however, and known in France as *garde robe* (clothes preserver) for just this reason. It is believed to have been introduced to Britain in the sixteenth century by French Huguenots, who were adept at creating the newly fashionable parterres and knot gardens. The shrubby herb was frequently selected as a hedging plant in the complex designs for it quickly establishes itself as a dense, low-growing hedge. Its silvery colour made it a wonderful foil for the plants it enclosed.

A hardy shrub, cotton lavender can grow 50cm (20in) high. The many-branched stems carry woolly-textured silvery or grey-green leaves. Sulphur-yellow flowers are borne in mid- to late summer, but it is the foliage that makes this plant so attractive and a popular garden plant.

Pick leaves for drying before flowering commences. The flowers can be dried for arranging. Tie them into small bunches and hang these upside down to dry in a well-ventilated room.

Cultivation

Cotton lavender enjoys well-drained sandy soil in full sun. As this is not an easy plant to grow from seed, it is preferable to take stem cuttings in spring or between mid-summer and autumn. The new plants root very easily, but give later cuttings protection over winter. Plant out in spring at 60cm (2ft) intervals. Tidy up the shape in spring and cut back again after flowering to stop plants becoming straggly. To cultivate a hedge, plant at 30cm (12in) intervals.

Medicinal use

Cotton lavender is infrequently used as a medicinal herb, although the leaves, if finely ground, are reputed to ease the pain caused by insect bites and stings. A decoction of the leaves can help cure ringworm if applied as a compress.

Home and beauty

This plant is an effective insect repellent. Make up herb bags and place in wardrobes and drawers to deter moths. Other herbs can be mixed with cotton lavender for this purpose; a typical cocktail might include rosemary, lavender and wormwood (*Artemisia*).

SAVORY

Savory is a powerful and bitter herb that enhances the flavour of food. It is believed to be one of the earliest-employed flavouring herbs and the Romans used it extensively in their cooking. Also regarded as an effective disinfectant, it was used as a strewing herb and burnt on fires to purify the atmosphere. It was also believed that it could cure frigidity and impotence. The ancient Egyptians used it in love potions and its generic name is derived from the Latin *satyrus*, which means 'satyr', a mythical lustful creature. Savory is now cultivated for the perfume industry and is used in the distillation of wines and spirits.

Summer savory (*Satureja hortensis*) is an aromatic hardy annual that grows 30cm (12in) high. The opposing leaves are narrow, pointed and dark green in colour. The small white, pink or purple flowers, which bloom in mid-summer, are very attractive to bees. Winter savory (*S. montana*), a hardy perennial that endures cold winters, is very similar in appearance to summer savory.

Use summer savory leaves fresh as required. For drying, pick all the leaves before flowering commences.

Cultivation

Savory enjoys a light rich soil in a sunny spot. Sow seed directly into the ground and thin seedlings to 20cm (8in) apart. Winter savory can be propagated from softwood cuttings taken in spring; plant out after roots have formed. This plant will self-seed in the right conditions.

Culinary use

Savory imparts its own strong flavour – spicy, warm and peppery – while drawing out the flavour of other ingredients, so must be used with a light hand. Summer savory has a lighter flavour than winter savory and is the herb generally recommended for culinary purposes. In France savory is commonly used in bean dishes, notably broad beans. It is also an important flavouring ingredient in salami. Savory is commonly used with food that is hard to digest.

Medicinal use

Savory is a digestive aid and a diuretic. It helps balance the digestive system, calming stomach cramps and wind. Savory is also reputed to be beneficial for treating gout and rheumatism. The crushed leaves are said to soothe wasp and bee stings quickly and effectively.

BROAD BEAN SOUP WITH SAVORY CREAM

Serves 4

25g (1oz) butter

2 onions, finely chopped

1 garlic clove, crushed

1tsp summer savory leaves

450g (1lb) shelled broad beans

1.1litres (2pints) hot vegetable stock

For the savory cream

150ml (¼pint) extra thick double cream
    or crème fraîche

2tsp freshly chopped summer savory,
    plus extra leaves to garnish

1 Melt the butter in a large pan, add the onions and cook gently for 7–8min until very soft but not coloured. Stir in the garlic and savory and cook for 1min.

2 Add the broad beans and stock, bring to the boil, cover and simmer for 15min until the beans are very tender.

3 Whiz the soup in batches in a food processor or liquidiser until smooth. Return to the pan and season to taste.

4 To make the savory cream, put the cream or crème fraîche in a bowl, stir in the chopped savory and season with salt and freshly ground black pepper.

5 Ladle the soup into warmed bowls, add a spoonful of the savory cream and serve, sprinkled with a few extra savory leaves.

ALEXANDERS, BLACK LOVAGE

Alexanders, or black lovage, was an important culinary herb for centuries and was listed as far back as BC322 by the Greek botanist Theophrastus. The botanical name is derived from the Greek for myrrh and alludes to its curiously sweet, perfumed flavour. The plant is similar to lovage, but bears black fruit, hence one of its common names. The Romans introduced the plant to Britain and sailors ate the dried leaves to help prevent scurvy. A popular potherb, it lost favour in the eighteenth century. However, this herb has much culinary merit and is so easy to grow it deserves to be more widely cultivated and used. It is indigenous to southern Europe but now grows freely across the continent and is commonly found growing in hedgerows and on waste ground.

A tall hardy biennial, alexanders can grow 1.5m (5ft) high. The large, serrated green leaves are topped by tall flower stems, which carry attractive green-yellow flowers from mid-spring to early summer. These are succeeded by small black fruit. The plant is often confused with angelica and lovage.

Harvest leaves and stems to use fresh or to dry before flowering commences.

Cultivation

Smyrnium is easy to cultivate. It enjoys a rich, moist soil in full sun or partial shade. Sow seed in autumn in a prepared garden site. Transplant young plants to their final position in spring.

Culinary use

All parts of this herb are edible. The shoots and leaves taste like a strong blend of celery and parsley but with perfumed overtones. Young shoots can be lightly cooked or used raw in salads. Mature stems can be added to sauces and stews as flavouring. The roots can be cooked as any other root vegetable, although I have not tried them myself. The seeds have a peppery flavour and can be substituted for pepper. I have used the leaves to replace lovage in nettle soup and gather it from the hedgerows.

Medicinal use

Smyrnium is a useful digestive. It also has mild diuretic, laxative and calmative properties.

COMFREY

For many centuries, comfrey was one of the foremost medicinal herbs. It is a powerful herb and still in use today. The botanical name comes from the Greek *sympho*, which means 'to unite' and alludes to the plant's supposed ability to heal broken bones. It was widely used to heal wounds, cuts, ulcers, bruises and sprains. The plant is indigenous to Europe and temperate Asia and it is believed that it was the Crusaders who discovered its healing powers. It became a feature of medieval herb gardens and was a key herb for Elizabethan physicians.

Comfrey is also highly valued by organic gardeners as a natural compost activator and a rich source of fertiliser. When added to a compost heap it activates the rapid breakdown of other compost materials. It is rich in nitrogen and makes a useful organic fertiliser (*see page 24*), although as this utilises a lot of leaves a home-grown supply is usually called for.

A tall spreading perennial, comfrey grows to 1m (3ft). It has large, coarse leaves and spikes of cream or blue flowers from late spring to early autumn.

Harvest leaves in early to mid-summer for drying. Store in an airtight container. Dig up roots from mid-autumn to early spring for drying. Splitting them lengthways will accelerate the drying process. Store in an airtight container.

Cultivation
Comfrey enjoys moist soil in sun or semi-shade. It is difficult to grow from seed, but very easy to propagate by division or root cuttings in spring. To make root cuttings, cut a section of root into 2cm (¾in) chunks and pot up; plant out when rooting has occurred.

Culinary use
Fresh comfrey leaves and shoots are very tasty, however as current research indicates that the plant may have carcinogenic properties if ingested, it is not advisable to consume the herb until more information is available.

Medicinal use
The herb has many medicinal properties and is currently the subject of much scientific research. It contains valuable vitamins, proteins, alkaloids, tannins and mucilage. However, the research also indicates that comfrey may have carcinogenic properties, although this applies only when the herb is taken internally. It is still a safe herb to use externally. Comfrey compresses, made from the fresh root or powdered dried root mixed with water, are soothing to sprains, bruises, burns and inflamed joints.

Home and beauty
Infusions made from the root are said to soften and soothe the skin.

FEVERFEW

In spite of its common name, feverfew does not appear to have any properties that could regulate temperature, but it was formerly in common use as a treatment for nervous disorders, such as melancholy, vertigo and arthritis. It was also used to soothe earache and applied as a poultice to relieve the pain of insect bites and stings. The herb has also long been regarded as an effective treatment for migraine and is the subject of much scientific research. As long ago as 1772, the herbalist J. Hill observed that 'in the worst headache there is no more efficacious remedy' than feverfew.

The herb is indigenous to southern Europe, but has naturalised around the world and is often found growing wild on wasteland and along roadsides. It is a hardy perennial herb and grows 60cm (2ft) high. The bright green aromatic leaflets are topped by numerous daisy-like button flower heads that bloom freely from late spring right through to late autumn.

To harvest, pick leaves for drying or freezing before flowering commences. Pick flowers for drying when they are newly opened; tie them into small bunches and hang these upside down in a well-ventilated room.

Cultivation

Feverfew is an easy plant to grow. It is tolerant of most soils and situations, but prefers a rich soil in a sunny position. Sow seed in a seed tray in spring or autumn and plant out when large enough to handle. Alternatively, sow directly into the ground in late spring and thin to 30cm (12in) apart. Lift and divide established clumps in early autumn. Feverfew self-seeds freely.

Medicinal use

Many migraine sufferers have found that taking feverfew reduces the frequency of attacks, although it is not yet understood precisely how the herb is beneficial. Between three and five leaves need to be consumed daily over several months before any improvement will occur. As the leaves taste extremely bitter and can cause mouth ulceration, it is advisable to take the herb sandwiched between two slices of bread. Use three to five leaves in a single sandwich and consume daily.

Home and beauty

Feverfew leaves can be put into herb bags to help to keep moths away from clothes. Lay the bags in drawers or hang them in wardrobes.

DANDELION

The dandelion is a well-known plant, more commonly regarded as a troublesome weed than as a useful herb. However, it has diuretic, laxative and digestive properties and is rich in vitamins, minerals, protein and sugar. The common name comes from the French *dent de lion*, meaning 'lion's tooth', and is thought to refer to the jagged-edge shape of the leaves. Confusingly, the French have another name altogether for the dandelion. They call it *pissenlit*, which literally means 'piss in bed' and is thought to allude to the plant's diuretic properties. In the late nineteenth century the dandelion was cultivated in cold houses by the well to do for use in winter salads, and during the Second World War radio broadcasts recommended it for culinary use.

Dandelion is a low-growing hardy perennial, naturalised in temperate regions across the world. The rosettes of the distinctively shaped leaves can be found in all but the coldest of months. The yellow flowers, which bloom from mid-spring to early autumn, are succeeded by the familiar seed heads.

Pick leaves for use fresh as required and the flowers for home brewing as soon as they open. Roots can be dug up in the autumn for drying.

Cultivation

Most people do not have to go the trouble of cultivating dandelions – like it or not they will come to you. However, the problem with using existing garden stock is that the leaves can become overly bitter with age. So to ensure a regular supply of fresh young leaves at their best for culinary use it is a good idea to cultivate the plant as an annual. Blanching the leaves makes them less bitter; place a pot over a plant to shut out the light and leave for seven days before harvesting.

Culinary use

Dandelion roots are said to provide a good caffeine-free substitute for coffee. Dig up the roots in autumn, clean them thoroughly then roast in the oven until quite brittle. The root can then be ground and used as one would coffee. The young leaves are very tasty mixed into salads. Blanched leaves taste less bitter than green ones, and in France they are served as a salad with bacon. Fresh young leaves are also tasty between thin slices of brown bread. More mature leaves can be cooked in a little butter and served with an olive oil and lemon juice dressing. The flowers can be made into dandelion wine, and dandelion and burdock was once a popular drink.

Medicinal use

The dandelion is regarded as helpful in the treatment of liver complaints. It is also claimed to be helpful for treating corns, warts and verrucas; simply bash the leaves about until they release liquid then rub them over the affected area.

DANDELION, BACON AND CROÛTON SALAD

Serves 4

225g (8oz) rashers of rindless
  streaky bacon
4 slices of ciabatta, cut into 2cm
  (¾in) cubes
1tbsp olive oil
1 level tsp Dijon mustard
2tbsp white wine vinegar
4tbsp extra virgin olive oil
4 medium eggs
125g (4oz) young dandelion leaves,
  washed and dried

1 Preheat the oven to 180°C (160°C in a fan oven), mark 4. Preheat the grill to high. Grill the bacon for 2–3min each side until crisp and golden. Cool on kitchen paper, then snap into small pieces.

2 Put the bread cubes in a bowl with the oil and toss together well. Spread over a baking sheet and bake for 8–10min until crisp and golden. Remove; leave to cool.

3 To make the dressing, mix the mustard and half of the vinegar together in a small bowl. Gradually whisk in the extra virgin olive oil then season well with salt and freshly ground black pepper.

4 Add the rest of the vinegar to a large pan of simmering water. Break one egg into a cup, stir the simmering water once or twice to create a whirlpool, then add the egg. Poach for 3min. Repeat with the remaining eggs. Remove with a slotted spoon; drain briefly on kitchen paper.

5 To serve, divide the dandelion leaves between four large plates and put a poached egg into the centre of each. Sprinkle over the bacon and croûtons, drizzle over the mustard dressing and serve straightaway.

THYME

bouquet garni

1 sprig of thyme

1 bay leaf

3 fresh parsley stalks

1 Put all the herbs in a muslin bag and tie securely. Alternatively, stuff the herbs in a leek or celery stalk and tie with string.

There are around a hundred species of thyme, but *Thymus vulgaris*, or garden thyme, is the favoured culinary herb. The name is derived from the Greek *thymus*, which means 'courage', or *thymon*, which means 'to fumigate'. The plant is indigenous to the Mediterranean region, where ancient civilisations made good use of it: the Egyptians utilised its antiseptic properties in their embalming oils; the Greeks added it to their baths to boost strength and energy; and the Romans used it to purify their rooms. In the Middle Ages the nobility carried thyme posies to ward off germs and mask unpleasant odours. At the same time the herb was adopted as a symbol of courage and was often seen as an emblem on knights' clothing. Thyme is undoubtedly a powerful antiseptic; the essential oil is 20 times stronger than phenol, the standard antiseptic, which explains its age-old popularity as a medicinal herb. It is also said to be a general tonic and a stimulant.

Thyme is a low-growing, bushy, evergreen aromatic herb that grows a mere 8–30cm (3–12in) high. It has tiny, oval, grey-green leaves and flowers that range in shade from red, through pink to white in early and mid-summer. It is an excellent plant for growing in cracks between paving where it will form a neat mound, but is equally attractive in pots.

You can pick thyme fresh all year round. However, if you want to preserve it pick the leaves for drying before the plant flowers.

Cultivation

As thyme is a drought-loving plant, it is imperative that it is planted in well-drained soil to get the best flavour from the leaves. It prefers a sunny sheltered spot in poor soil and needs protection from cold and wet winters. Trim plants after flowering to encourage new growth and to stop the plant becoming woody. Propagate thyme from softwood cuttings taken in early spring or summer or by division. The herb can be grown from seed, but is inclined to hybridise easily so great care must be taken to keep different varieties separate if you wish to use this method.

Culinary use

Thyme is a popular culinary herb. It has a strong flavour so should be used with discretion. It is an essential ingredient of *bouquet garni*, the classic herb mix used to season stews and soup. Thyme can be used to flavour vinegar and oil, both of which can make wonderful marinades. As the herb helps break down fatty foods, it is a popular ingredient in stuffings for rich meats and fish. Lemon thyme (*T.* x *citriodorus*) is a related species, whose thyme flavour is enhanced by lemony overtones; it makes an interesting alternative culinary herb and is delicious with chicken.

Medicinal use

The thymol content of thyme makes it a natural antiseptic. It is therefore an effective treatment for sore throats and infected gums, and is helpful for easing respiratory infections, such as colds, coughs and influenza. It is also thought to be useful for treating bladder infections. The herb is still commonly used in the manufacture of toothpaste and mouthwash. It is also said to ease rheumatic pain and is often included in massage oils. A few drops of the essential oil in bath water will help heal cuts and grazes. Thyme aids digestion and eases flatulence A night-time cup of thyme tea, sweetened with a little honey, is said to induce sleep; tea made from lemon thyme is especially delicious. Thyme tea is also thought to be an effective remedy for candida. Strong thyme teas should not be used during pregnancy, however.

Home and beauty

For a soothing and relaxing bath simply add a few drops of thyme essential oil to the water.

COURGETTE AND THYME TART

Serves 6

2tbsp olive oil

1 bunch of spring onions, sliced

350g (12oz) courgettes, roughly chopped

1 level tbsp small sprigs of thyme

300g (11oz) medium-fat soft goats' cheese

3 medium eggs

200ml (7fl oz) double cream

125g (4oz) feta cheese, roughly chopped

175g (6oz) packet ready-made shortcrust
    pastry, chilled

1 In a large frying pan, heat the olive oil, add the spring onions and cook for 1–2min. Add the courgettes and cook for a further 2–3min. Season with salt and freshly ground black pepper and add the thyme. Turn into a wide bowl to cool.

2 In a large bowl, mix together the goats' cheese, two of the eggs, cream, feta cheese and the cooled courgettes. Set aside in a cool place.

3 Roll the pastry out thinly on a lightly floured surface, and line a 23cm (9in) loose-bottomed flan tin; chill for 20min.

4 Preheat the oven to 200ºC (180ºC in a fan oven), mark 6. Line the pastry case with greaseproof paper and fill with baking beans. Cook for 15min, remove the paper and baking beans and cook for a further 5min until the pastry is dry to the touch. Allow to cool for 5min, brush the inside of the pastry case with the remaining beaten egg and return it to the oven for 4–5min or until the egg has formed a seal. Pour in the courgette and cheese mixture and cook for 30–35min or until the filling is just set.

5 Leave the tart to cool for 5min then carefully unmould it on to a cooling rack. Serve it warm or cold with a dressed green salad.

NASTURTIUM

Bright, cheerful and easy to grow, the nasturtium is a well-loved cottage garden favourite with the bonus of being packed with vitamins and minerals. Indigenous to South America, it was introduced to Europe in the sixteenth century by the Spanish. The herb is reputed to cleanse the blood and promote digestion and was eaten to prevent scurvy. It is a useful companion plant because it attracts hoverflies, which prey on aphids. It is also reputed to deter ants and can be planted under fruit trees to keep pests like woolly aphids at bay.

The nasturtium is a hardy annual climber that can grow 1–3m (3–10ft) high. However, heights can vary enormously as different varieties and hybrids climb, trail or sprawl. The plant has flat, round leaves and flame-coloured flower trumpets from early summer until the first frosts of autumn.

Pick leaves and flowers for use fresh as required. Harvest the seeds for pickling whilst they are still fresh and green.

Cultivation

Nasturtiums enjoy well-drained soil in full sun or semi-shade, but for a good show of flowers the soil needs to be poor. They are easily grown from seed, and can be sown in pots or directly into the ground, 20cm (8in) apart, when the temperatures begin to rise in spring. Given the right conditions nasturtiums will self-seed freely. They are good plants for growing in containers.

 Culinary use

Nasturtiums are a tasty herb and contain vitamin C and iron. All parts of the plant are edible. The leaves and flowers have a peppery flavour and are tasty in salads and sandwiches. The flowers, which are milder in flavour than the leaves, make an interesting addition to a salad. The seeds and flower buds can be pickled; their taste is not dissimilar to that of capers. Like sorrel, the nasturtium contains oxalic acid, which can lead to the formation of tiny stones of calcium oxolate, so do not eat very much of this plant at any one time.

Medicinal use

The herb is thought to be a tonic for the digestive system and can help relieve constipation. It is also said to have antibiotic properties.

PAN-FRIED DOVER SOLE WITH NASTURTIUM SEED AND NUT BROWN BUTTER

Serves 2

25g (1oz) plain flour

2 x 400–450g (14oz–1lb) Dover soles,
    cleaned and skinned

2tbsp sunflower oil

50g (2oz) salted butter

1tbsp pickled nasturtium seeds, drained
    and rinsed

2tsp lemon juice

1tbsp freshly chopped flat-leaf parsley

1 Season the flour with ½tsp salt and some freshly ground black pepper. Coat each Dover sole on both sides with the seasoned flour, then knock off the excess.
2 Heat half of the oil in a large frying pan. Add 15g (½oz) of the butter and as soon as it starts to foam, add one of the fish and fry over a medium heat for 4–5min until golden brown.
3 Carefully turn the fish over and continue to cook for 4–5min until golden brown and cooked through. Lift on to a serving plate and keep warm. Cook the other fish in the same way.
4 Drain any frying oil from the pan and wipe clean. Add the remaining butter to the pan and melt it over a medium heat. When the butter has turned light brown and starts to smell nutty, add the nasturtium seeds, lemon juice and parsley. Pour some of this flavoured butter over each fish and serve immediately.

STINGING NETTLE

nettle tea

2tsp freshly chopped nettle leaves

1 Boil some water and pour into a cup, add the chopped nettles and leave to infuse for 4–5min.
2 Strain the liquid and discard the nettle before drinking.
→ Drink 1 cup up to three times a day to cleanse the system. It also helps in the treatment of asthma, hay fever and some skin allergies

nettle rinse

handful of fresh nettle leaves

1 Put the nettles in a pan and pour in 600ml (1pint) water. Bring to the boil then simmer very gently, covered, for 15min.
2 Strain the liquid and discard the leaves. Allow to cool before using.
→ Pour over the head as a final rinse after shampooing. The rinse will not keep for long so use it liberally and make a fresh mix as required.

The stinging nettle is commonly found in temperate regions throughout the world and is probably the most common wild herb. It has a long history of use in the kitchen as well as in home brewing. It is rich in vitamins A and C, as well as iron and other minerals and is believed to act as a tonic and purify the system. Medicinally, nettles are used to treat a range of conditions from dandruff to arthritis. The coarse fibres from the stalks have been used in the past to make cloth, rope and paper. Nettle-fibre cloth was found wrapped around a body dating from the late Bronze Age. In spite of the plant's stinging deterrent, its very abundance has made it an important food source in times of shortage – it was widely eaten during both the potato famine and the Second World War. It is the hairs in the nettle that sting, each hair being a brittle hollow needle; the point breaks easily on touch, which releases the formic acid inside. The cooking process destroys the formic acid rendering the greens safe to eat.

The stinging nettle is a perennial herb that can grow up to 1.2m (4ft) high. The toothed and veined oval leaves are covered with stinging hairs. Insignificant green flowers appear throughout summer, lasting until the beginning of autumn.

Pick leaves for use fresh as required. For culinary use, pick them before flowering commences. Always wear protective gloves when handling nettles.

Cultivation

As there is no shortage of supply in town or country, stinging nettles are best gathered form the wild. The plant enjoys nitrogen-rich soil, so a patch of nettles indicates good fertile land. If you can tolerate a clump in your own garden they do attract butterflies and moths.

Culinary use

Although this herb has few culinary uses, do not underestimate it. It is packed full of vitamins and minerals, but remember that only fresh young leaves should be used. Nettle soup is deliciously mild. Serve it to guests and keep them guessing until their bowls are empty! Wear gloves to pick the nettles and remove the leaves from the stalks.

Medicinal use

Stinging nettles are a digestive, a diuretic and an astringent. As the herb is rich in both iron and vitamin C, which ensures the ready absorption of the iron by the body, it is useful for treating anaemia. It is also reputed to be helpful for treating rheumatism and arthritis. The traditional treatment for these ailments involves brushing the affected joint with the plant until it is covered with stings. After this torture the joint should be kept mobile for 30 minutes. The process should be repeated over time until the joints are no longer painful. Nettles also contain histamine so a tea may alleviate some of the symptoms of hay fever and skin allergies. Nettle tea is also reputed to be a good detoxifier.

Home and beauty

A nettle rinse is reputed to help eradicate dandruff and to leave hair shiny and soft. As the leaves are astringent they can also be used in facial steams to tone the skin; place a handful of young leaves in a bowl and pour over boiling water.

NETTLE SOUP

50g (2oz) butter
1 onion, roughly chopped
225g (8oz) potatoes, peeled and roughly
    chopped
225g (8oz) young nettle leaves, washed
    and dried
600ml (1pint) milk
1tsp freshly chopped sweet marjoram
1dssp freshly chopped lovage

1 Heat the butter in a large pan, add the onion and cook gently until soft and translucent.
2 Add the chopped potatoes and nettles, cover and cook gently for 10min.
3 Pour the milk into the pan and add the marjoram and lovage. Bring gently to the boil, reduce the heat and simmer for 10min.
4 Leave the soup to cool a little then pour into a food processor and liquidise. Put back in the pan and heat gently to serve.

HEARTSEASE

heartsease decoction

15g (½oz) dried heartsease flowers

1 Pour 900ml (1½pints) cold water into a pan, add the heartsease and set aside to infuse for 1hr.

2 Heat the liquid and remove from the heat the moment it comes to the boil. Set aside for 5min.

3 Strain the liquid and discard the heartsease before drinking or using.

➔ Drink up to 900ml (1½pints) a day to treat rheumatism or exhaustion. Alternatively, use as a lotion for skin complaints.

A parent of the showier modern pansy, heartsease is an unassuming little plant that carries the sweetest of flowers. As the common name suggests, this herb has long been associated with love and romance, a reputation which may, in part, have originated from its medicinal use as a treatment for heart and blood disorders. During the Middle Ages heartsease was also popularly known as the herb of trinity because there are three colours in every flower.

Heartsease is indigenous to Europe and western Asia. It is an annual or short-lived perennial and grows 30cm (12in) high. It carries oval green leaves and delicate violet, yellow and white flowers that bloom throughout the summer. The multi-coloured flower carries four petals above and one below, which gives it the appearance of a cheerful little bonneted face.

To harvest heartsease, pick the flowers throughout the flowering season when they are fully open – midday is usually best. Use them fresh or dried. Store dried flowers in an airtight glass jar, where they will still look very pretty.

Cultivation
Heartsease is a tolerant plant that will grow in sun or semi-shade. Sow seeds from spring to autumn directly into the ground. The plant will self-seed in the most unexpected places. Deadhead throughout the summer to extend the flowering period. Heartsease makes an excellent container plant.

Culinary use
Heartsease flowers can be mixed into salads to add colour.

Medicinal use
Heartsease is a mild diuretic; it helps eradicate toxins from the body and is said to stimulate the metabolism. It is used to treat skin complaints, notably infant eczema, and is said to relieve rheumatism. It is also reputed to help cure bed-wetting.

SWEET VIOLET

violet infusion

5g (¼oz) dried violet flowers

1 Pour 900ml (1½pints) water into a pan, add the dried violet flowers and leave for 3min.
2 Bring the liquid to the boil, remove from the heat and set aside to infuse for 5min.
3 Strain the liquid and discard the flowers before drinking.
➔ Use externally as required or drink 1 cup up to three times a day.

The violet is a diminutive little flower with a powerful and instantly recognisable fragrance. It is indigenous to Europe and North Africa. The ancient Greeks made it their symbol of fertility and it was the designated flower of both Aphrodite, the goddess of love, and her son Priapus, the god of gardens. Napoleon adopted the flower as the emblem for his imperial Napoleonic party. Later, so many Victorian ladies wore tiny bunches of violets as corsages that the flower was heavily cultivated to meet the demand. Violets have been used extensively through history to make perfume and are still used today; over 100kg (220lb) of flowers are required to extract just 50g (2oz) of essence. Violets also have medicinal value. A tenth-century herbal shows that early Britons mixed violets with goat's milk to make a skin lotion. The herb was a traditional treatment for headaches, which may in part be due to the fact that it contains salicylic acid, from which aspirin is derived.

A creeping hardy perennial, the violet grows 15cm (6in) high. It has attractive heart-shaped leaves and fragile, highly perfumed purple flowers that are borne on delicate stems through spring. The flowers have three petals above and two below.

Collect leaves in early spring and flowers when newly opened for drying. Dry in an airy room out of direct daylight so that colour and fragrance are preserved. Store in airtight containers – they will look pretty in glass jars.

Cultivation

A tolerant plant, the violet will grow almost anywhere, although it is happiest in partial shade. Sow seed in trays in autumn and keep under glass throughout the winter, or sow directly into the ground in spring. Established plants can be lifted and divided. The violet will self-seed freely given the right conditions.

Culinary use

The violet has very little culinary use, but the flowers can be crystallised to make cake decorations (*see page 44*).

Medicinal use

Violets are a purgative and a laxative. Both a tea made from the leaves and/or flowers and a syrup made from the flowers can be used to relieve bronchial complaints. However, syrup requires a lot of flowers – about 150g (5oz).

Home and beauty

Violet infusions can soothe tired and swollen eyes. Soak cotton pads in a cooled infusion then lie down. Lay the pads on the eyes and rest for 15–20 minutes. The fragrant dried flowers can be added to potpourri.

A-Z of Herbs

Herb	Site	Sow/Propagate	Harvest
Achillea millefolium (Yarrow)	Tolerant	Autumn	Start of flowering
Allium sativum (Garlic)	Sunny	Autumn	Summer
Allium schoenoprasum (Chives)	Sun, partial shade	Spring	Before flowering
Aloysia triphylla (Lemon verbena)	Sunny: tender, protect in winter	Spring	Before and during flowering
Althaea officinalis (Marsh mallow)	Sunny, moist soil	Autumn	When in leaf
Anethum graveolens (Dill)	Sunny	Spring	When in leaf, seed in late summer
Angelica archangelica (Angelica)	Partial shade, moist soil	Autumn	When in leaf and flower, seed in late summer
Anthriscus cerefolium (Chervil)	Semi-shade, moist soil	Late spring	Throughout summer
Armoracia rusticana (Horseradish)	Sunny	Spring	Autumn
Artemisia dracunculus (Tarragon)	Sunny	Spring	Throughout summer
Atriplex hortensis (Orach)	Partial shade	Late spring	Throughout summer
Borago officinalis (Borage)	Sunny	Spring/autumn	Throughout summer
Brassica (Mustard)	Sunny	Spring and onwards	Throughout summer
Calendula officinalis (Pot marigold)	Sunny	Spring	Throughout summer
Carum carvi (Caraway)	Sun, partial shade	Autumn	Throughout summer
Chamaemelum nobile (Chamomile)	Sunny	Spring	Throughout summer
Cichorium intybus (Chicory)	Sunny	Spring/summer	Late summer/autumn
Coriandrum sativum (Coriander)	Sunny	Spring	Throughout summer
Eruca vesicaria (Rocket)	Light shade	Spring and onwards	Throughout summer
Filipendula ulmaria (Meadowsweet)	Partial shade	Autumn	Before and during flowering
Foeniculum vulgare (Fennel)	Sunny	Spring	Throughout summer
Fragaria vesca (Wild strawberry)	Sun, light shade	Spring	Throughout summer
Galium odoratum (Sweet woodruff)	Dry shade	Autumn	Early summer
Glycyrrhiza glabra (Liquorice)	Sun, light shade	Spring/autumn	Harvest roots after 3–4 years
Hamamelis virginiana (Witchhazel)	Sun, light shade	Autumn	As required
Humulus lupulus (Hop)	Sunny	Spring	Throughout growing season
Hyssopus officinalis (Hyssop)	Sunny	Spring	Summer
Juniperus communis (Juniper)	Sunny	Spring	End of summer
Laurus nobilis (Sweet bay)	Sunny	Spring	All year
Lavandula angustifolia (Lavender)	Sunny	Autumn	Summer
Levisticum officinale (Lovage)	Sunny, moist soil	Spring	Throughout summer
Malus sylvestris (Crab apple)	Sunny	Autumn	Autumn
Melissa officinalis (Lemon balm)	Sunny	Spring	Throughout summer
Mentha (Mint)	Sun, light shade	Spring	Throughout summer
Monarda (Bergamot)	Semi-shade	Spring	Leaves before flowering, flowers as required

Culinary use	Used to treat
In salads and dips	Fevers and wounds
Essential flavouring	Cholesterol and high blood pressure, chest and fungus infections
Essential flavouring	Mildly antibiotic and antifungal, aids digestion stimulates appetite
Herb oil and vinegar	Nausea, indigestion and flatulence
Root as vegetable	Inflammation and ulceration of stomach and intestine
Essential flavouring	Soothing, calming digestive, eases colic in babies
Leaf as flavouring, stem for cake decoration	Flatulence and indigestion
Essential flavouring	Mild diuretic, aids digestion
Hot flavouring for sauces and dips	Acts as diuretic, stimulates circulation, soothes rheumatism and chilblains
Essential flavouring	Digestive upsets, rheumatism and arthritis
Leaf as vegetable, in soups	Indigestion and hysteria
Chopped leaf in salad, flowers in fruit cups	Temperatures, also soothing and anti-inflammatory
Mustard made from seeds, leaves and flowers in salads	Relieves inflammation and pain applied as poultice
Flower petals in salads, omelettes and puddings	Promotes healing, soothing with antibacterial, antiseptic and antifungal properties
Seeds for baking, leaves in salads	Digestive properties and sweetens the breath
Tea as a calmative	Eases nausea and insomnia, soothing to stomach complaints
Chicons and flowers in salads, root as vegetable	A mild diuretic, soothes inflammation of the urinary tract, the gall bladder and the liver
Essential flavouring in soups, stews, curries and sauces	Seeds are a digestive and will stimulate appetite
Young leaves in salads	Rich in minerals and vitamins, a tonic
Flavouring for stewed fruit and jam, herb vinegar	Diarrhoea, also colds and influenza
Flavouring for marinades and stuffing, root as vegetable	Indigestion, constipation and cystitis
In desserts and cakes or for jam	Anaemia, stomach upsets and nerves
Flavouring for German May punch, relaxing tea	Soothes stomach ache, mild diuretic
Flavouring for beer and confectionery	Relieves indigestion and stomach complaints, soothes coughs
	Soothes insect bites, cuts, bruises and sprains, powerful astringent
Young shoots as vegetable like asparagus	Acts as sedative and soporific
Strong flavouring for sauces and stuffing	Sore throats, coughs and bruising
Flavouring for rich meat	Urinary tract infections, bronchial complaints, indigestion, diuretic
Essential flavouring	Stimulates the appetite and aids digestion
Flavouring for biscuits and ice cream	Soothes burns, stings and headaches, anti-inflammatory
Flavouring for stocks and stews, as vegetable	Soothes digestive complaints, stimulates the appetite, mild diuretic
For jellies, pickles and home brewing	A cleansing fruit, stimulates digestion, helps balance cholesterol
Replaces lemongrass and lemon rind, delicious tea	Has soothing and sedative properties, relieves headaches
Essential flavouring	Antispasmodic, anti-inflammatory, antibacterial, aids digestion
Delicious tea	Soothes upset stomach, relieves period pain

Herb	Site	Sow/Propagate	Harvest
Myrrhis odorata (Sweet cicely)	Light shade	Autumn	Throughout summer
Myrtus communis (Myrtle)	Sunny	Summer	All year
Nepeta (Catmint)	Sunny	Spring, late summer	Summer
Ocimum basilicum (Basil)	Sunny	Spring.	Summer
Oenothera biennis (Evening primrose)	Sunny	Late-spring	Summer
Origanum (Marjoram and Oregano)	Sunny	Early spring	Throughout growing season
Papaver (Poppy)	Sunny	Spring, autumn	Late summer
Pelargonium (Scented-leaved geranium)	Sunny	Spring, late summer	Throughout growing season
Petroselinum crispum (Parsley)	Sun, semi-shade	Spring	Throughout growing season
Primula veris (Cowslip)	Semi-shade	Autumn	Spring
Primula vulgaris (Primrose)	Partial shade	Autumn	Spring
Prunus spinosa (Blackthorn, sloe)	Tolerant	Autumn	Autumn
Rosa canina, R. gallica (Dog rose, Apothecary's rose)	Sun, semi-shade	Autumn	Summer and autumn
Rosmarinus officinalis (Rosemary)	Sunny	Summer	All year
Rubus fruticosus (Blackberry)	Sunny	Summer	Summer and autumn
Rumex (Sorrel)	Sun, partial shade	Late spring	Spring and onwards
Salvia officinalis (Sage)	Sunny	Late spring	All year
Sambucus nigra (Elder)	Sunny	Autumn	Late spring and autumn
Sanguisorba minor (Salad burnet)	Sun, partial shade	Spring	Throughout growing season
Santolina chamaecyparissus (Cotton lavender)	Sunny	Summer, autumn	Summer
Satureja (Savory)	Sunny	Spring	Leaves before flowering
Smyrnium olusatrum (Alexanders, black lovage)	Sun, partial shade	Autumn	Leaves before flowering
Symphytum officinale (Comfrey)	Sun, semi-shade	Spring	Summer and autumn
Tanaceteum parthenium (Feverfew)	Sunny	Spring, autumn	Leaves before flowering, flowers as required
Taraxacum officinale (Dandelion)	Tolerant	Spring	Summer and autumn
Thymus vulgaris (Thyme)	Sunny	Spring, summer	All year
Tropaeolum majus (Nasturtium)	Sun, semi-shade	Spring	Summer
Urtica dioica (Nettle)	Tolerant	Spring	Late spring
Viola tricolor (Heartsease)	Sun, semi-shade	Spring to autumn	Throughout growing season
Viola odorata (Violet)	Partial shade	Autumn	Spring

Culinary use	Used to treat
Leaves, seeds and root can be used	Acts as digestive, seeds relieve flatulence
Flavouring for rich meat	Chest complaints, antibiotic, antiseptic and astringent
	Mild sedative
Essential flavouring	Sedative and antispasmodic, relieves headaches
Flowerbuds and leaves are edible	PMS, eczema and arthritis
Essential flavouring	Soporific, sedative and digestive
Seed for baking	
Flavouring ice cream, cakes and drinks	Relieves PMS
Essential flavouring	Kidney, bladder and urinary tract infections, diuretic and antiseptic
Flowers in salads, home brewing and cake decoration	Bronchial complaints and arthritis, is antispasmodic and sedative
Flowers in salads and cake decoration	Sedative and expectorant
Sloe gin and sloe jelly	
Hips for jellies, petals for delicate flavouring	Cleansing tonic
Essential flavouring	Aids digestion and stimulates circulation, antibacterial and antifungal
Jellies and desserts	Diarrhoea, piles, cystitis
Fresh in salads, flavouring for sauces and soups	Diarrhoea and stomach upsets
Essential flavouring, herb oil and vinegar	Sore throats and indigestion, makes soothing poultice
Flavouring for summer drinks or home brewing	Colds and influenza, acts as anti-inflammatory
Leaves in salads, herb vinegar	Diarrhoea and haemorrhoids, a compress soothes headaches
	Soothes insect bites and stings
Flavouring for bean dishes and salami	Soothes wasp and bee stings, digestive and diuretic
All parts can be eaten	Digestive and calmative
	Sprains, bruises, burns and inflammation
	Migraines
Leaves in salads, lightly cooked, roasted root as coffee substitute	Diuretic and anti-inflammatory
Essential flavouring	Cuts, sore throats and infected gums, antiseptic
Leaves and flowers in salads	Constipation, antibiotic properties
Nutritious soup	Anaemia, rheumatism and arthritis
Flowers in salads	Stimulates metabolism and eradicates toxins
Flowers can be crystallised	A purgative and laxative

Bibliography

Bonar, Ann. *Herbs*. Hamlyn, 1985.

Boxer, Arabella. *The Herb Book*. Hamlyn, 1996.

Boxer, Arabella & Philippa Back. *The Herb Book*. Octopus Books, 1981.

Bremness, Lesley. *The Complete Book of Herbs*. Guild Publishing, 1990.

Bremness, Lesley. *Fragrant Herb Garden*. Quadrille, 2000.

Buchman, Dian Dincin. *Herbal Medicine*. The Herb Society/Rider, 1983.

Hall, Dorothy. *The Book of Herbs*. Angus and Robertson, 1972.

Hedley, Christopher & Non Shaw. *Herbal Remedies*. Parragon Book Service, 1996.

Hulme, F. Edward. *Wild Flowers in Their Seasons*. Cassell & Co Ltd. , 1907.

Mabey, Richard. *Flora Britannica Book of Wild Herbs*. Chatto & Windus, 1998.

Mabey, Richard. *Food for Free*. Collins, 1980.

McVicar, Jekka. *Jekka's Complete Herb Book*. Kyle Cathie Ltd, 1997.

Phillips, Roger & Nicky Foy. *Herbs*. Pan Books Ltd, 1990.

Pickston, Margaret. *The Language of Flowers*. Michael Joseph Ltd, 1968.

Potterton, David (Ed). *Culpepper's Colour Herbal*. Foulsham, 1997.

Rohde, Eleanour Sinclair. *Rose Recipes from Olden Times*. Dover Publications Inc., 1973.

Sanecki, Kay N. *History of the English Herb Garden*. Ward Lock, 1994.

Smith, Delia. *Complete Cookery Course*. BBC Books, 1982.

Smith, Keith Vincent. *The Illustrated Earth Garden Herbal*. Lothian, 1994.

Stickland, Sue. *Planning Your Organic Herb Garden*. Thorsons, 1986.

van Straten, Michael. *Super Herbs*. Mitchell Beazley, 2000.

Verey, Rosemary. *The Scented Garden*. Michael Joseph Ltd, 1981.

The Country Housewife's Book. West Kent Federation of Women's Institutes, 1968.

Food from your Garden. Readers Digest Association Ltd, 1985.

The Work of Dr Edward Bach. Wigmore Publications Ltd, 1995.

Reference

Brown, Deni. *RHS Encyclopedia of Herbs & Their Uses*. Dorling Kindersley, 1995.

Mitchell, Alan. *A Field Guide to the Trees of Britain and Northern Europe*. Collins, 1988.

Encyclopaedia of Garden Plants and Flowers. Reader's Digest, 1987.

The Royal Horticultural Society Encyclopaedia of Gardening. Dorling Kindersley, 1992.

Wild Flowers of Britain and Northern Europe. Collins, 1978.

Index

A page number in **bold** indicates the main entry for a herb in the *Herb Directory*. See the main entry for a description and photograph of the herb, and full information on its history, cultivation and uses. Page numbers in *italics* indicate recipes (both culinary and non-culinary).

picture credits

All photography supplied by Flowerphotos. Photographs are by Carol Sharp except: Richard Freestone p. 57; Grace Carlon pp. 75, 135; Michael Peuckert pp. 79 (rpt 50), 95; Barbara Gray p. 103; Roy Chatfield p. 107; Ewa Ohlsson p. 111; Mike Bentley p. 143; Dave Tully pp. 119, 149, Sarah McGibbon p. 161; Martin O'Neil pp. 173 (rpt 2) and Steve Shipman p.177.

author's acknowledgements

I would like to thank Sarah Gristwood for her support, Elizabeth Sheppard Jones for her inspiration and Philip Pelham and Susan Espley for their words of advice. Most of all I would like to thank my family: Eric for his healthy scepticism and our children Florence and Teddy for their enthusiasm, tolerance and good-natured compliance in hunting, gathering and testing the many herbal recipes and remedies. Lastly I would like to thank Katie Cowan and Polly Powell for their faith in me.

publisher's acknowledgements

All recipes are from the GHI Archives with the exception of those appearing on pages 75, 79, 103, 111, 153, 171 and 175, developed by Debbie Major. Thanks to Emma Marsden at Good Housekeeping for her help and advice on recipe selection. Special thanks to Monty and Bob for their constant help and support.

Editor	**Jackie Matthews**
Typist	**Liz Spicer**
Typesetter	**Michelle Pickering**
Proofreader	**Jo Lethaby**
Index	**Sue Bosanko**
Designer	**Liz Brown**
Illustrator	**Martine Collings**
Photograpy Stylist	**Susan Downing**